S0-AZR-516

At Issue

Media Bias and the Role of the Press

Other Books in the At Issue Series

At Issue

Media Bias and the Role of the Press

Eamon Doyle, Book Editor

GREENHAVEN
PUBLISHING

Published in 2019 by Greenhaven Publishing, LLC
353 3rd Avenue, Suite 255, New York, NY 10010

Copyright © 2019 by Greenhaven Publishing, LLC

First Edition

All rights reserved. No part of this book may be reproduced in any form
without permission in writing from the publisher, except by a reviewer.

Articles in Greenhaven Publishing anthologies are often edited for length to meet page
requirements. In addition, original titles of these works are changed to clearly present
the main thesis and to explicitly indicate the author's opinion. Every effort is made to
ensure that Greenhaven Publishing accurately reflects the original intent of the authors.
Every effort has been made to trace the owners of the copyrighted material.

Cover image: razorbeam/Shutterstock.com

Library of Congress Cataloging-in-Publication Data
Names: Doyle, Eamon.
Title: Media bias and the role of the press / Eamon Doyle, book editor.
Description: First edition. | New York : Greenhaven Publishing, 2019. |
  Series: At issue | Includes bibliographical references and index. | Audience: Grades 9–12.
Identifiers: LCCN 2018000503| ISBN 9781534503281 (library bound) | ISBN
  9781534503298 (pbk.)
Subjects: LCSH: Journalism—Objectivity—United States. | Mass
  media—Objectivity—United States. | Journalism—Political aspects—United
  States.
Classification: LCC PN4888.O25 M44 2018 | DDC 302.230973—dc23
LC record available at https://lccn.loc.gov/2018000503

Manufactured in the United States of America

Website: http://greenhavenpublishing.com

Contents

Introduction

In the modern era, the communication media environment has undergone a series of radical technological and business evolutions. These evolutions have transformed the fabric of daily life, carrying the civilized world all the way from the printing press to the iPhone. Over the course of this series of developments, the media sector has allowed for larger and larger societies to centralize their resources and share information seamlessly across time and geographic divides. Indeed, what we refer to as "the modern world" is largely defined by media innovations—the printed pamphlet, the radio, the telephone, the television, the computer, and the internet. Because of this deep connection between developments in the media sector and the structure of modern society as a whole, media topics often feature prominently in the political discourse.

In the United States, strong cultural traditions around individual choice and democratic elections stress the importance of citizens *making up their own minds* about political issues. Media skeptics worry that reporters and editors, influenced by their own ideological preferences, are liable to present information in a way that not only informs but persuades as well. This is often referred to as "media bias." Mainstream journalists and media professionals have generally adopted a proactive stance on the issue, employing specific language and sourcing techniques intended to increase the transparency of their work and cultivate trust with their audience. These tactics are considered to be part of "journalistic objectivity," a professional ethic shared by reporters and editors that speaks directly to fears of a biased, manipulative media landscape. Organizations such as the News Media Alliance, the American Press Institute, and the Society of Professional Journalists regularly publish resources to support and encourage reporters who adhere to journalistic objectivity.

Beginning in the middle of the twentieth century, the dominant media forms—print newspapers, radio, and television—all relied on significant production, broadcasting, and distribution infrastructure. The cost of this type of investment led to a national media environment characterized by consolidation and scale, and dominated by a few major players—CBS, NBC, and ABC on television; the *Wall Street Journal,* the *New York Times,* and the *Washington Post* in print. But there was a robust market for local print news as well, with most major cities supporting a small handful of regional papers. The television networks drew the majority of their profits from non-news, entertainment-based programming, and in general, profitability metrics were applied less stringently in news divisions.

The last quarter of a century has seen these dynamics beginning to shift. Corporate buyouts decimated a large number of local papers, and increased pressure to show profitability led many of the major news outlets to view their audience more as an entertainment market than as citizens trying to stay informed.[1] As a result, content started to be judged in editorial rooms by its ability to draw eyeballs rather than the quality of its reporting or its objectivity, which in turn often allowed more ideologically driven reporting to capitalize on the liberal and conservative "markets." For example, the Fox News television network was formed in the 1990s with the express purpose of countering the narratives promoted by perceived liberal outlets like the *New York Times* and CBS. This represented a major change from earlier in the century when most major news sources assumed that they were producing content for a mass audience.

And then came the internet. In the late 1990s and early 2000s, major news sources launched websites and began trying to find their way in the new digital media marketing environment. It has been a difficult transition for a variety of reasons. For example, a major portion of ad revenue for newspapers traditionally came from their classified listings. When Craigslist offered free online listings that could reach exponentially more people than print ads could, there was no easy way for the major print news outlets to compete. Additionally, revenue from traditional print advertising has shrunk dramatically as advertisers focus more on the online space. As a result of these net revenue losses, many newspapers have been forced to scale back their operations and lay off reporters.

On the flipside, online-based media outlets and aggregators have proliferated exponentially, and most Americans (two-thirds, according to Reuters[2]) now get their news via social media platforms like Facebook and Twitter, which distribute content based on algorithmic design. Some enthusiasts argue that competition and diversity of online news outlets represents a positive development in the media landscape—that more voices are being heard and more information is available than ever before. But critics worry that the unrestrained profusion of news sources will lead to ideological balkanization and confusion in the public discourse: "I am not sure it's possible to fully appreciate the implications of this sort of thing," writes *Vox* editor Ezra Klein, "Basically all democratic theory is built around the idea that people have a roughly accurate and shared view of what's going on. What if they don't?"[3]

In the wake of the 2016 presidential election, the tension between these perspectives arguably has become the single most important issue in American politics. Allegations of election interference involving fake news stories distributed on social media platforms are the subject of a major special counsel investigation that has already produced indictments and guilty pleas from key members of President Trump's campaign staff. Skepticism and distrust of the news media are on the rise among both citizens and professional political operatives, and some politicians appear to be comfortable using such dynamics to their advantage by dismissing inconvenient facts and coverage as "fake news." It is far from clear what the effects of this shift will be on the levels of politics, economics, and ideology. The best that many media experts seem to be able to offer in terms of a prediction is: *stay tuned.*

While much remains uncertain, the viewpoints presented in *At Issue: Media Bias and the Role of the Press* will provide analysis of the ways media in the United States has changed over the past century and whether these changes have contributed to media bias. Viewpoint authors will also explore the nature of media bias and discuss potential means of combatting it.

Notes

1. Gunther, Marc. "The Transformation of Network News: How Profitability Has Moved Networks Out of Hard News." *Nieman Reports.* June 15, 1999.

2. Moon, Angela. "Two-thirds of American Adults Get News from Social Media: Survey." Reuters. September 8, 2017. https://www.reuters.com/article/us-usa-internet-socialmedia/two-thirds-of-american-adults-get-news-from-social-media-survey-idUSKCN1BJ2A8.

3. Klein, Ezra. Twitter (@ezraklein). December 28, 2017. https://twitter.com/ezraklein/status/946533860946468866

1

Theoretical Foundations of News Media as a Source of Social and Political Power

Teun A. van Dijk

Teun A. van Dijk was a professor of discourse studies at the University of Amsterdam for over three decades. Currently, he teaches and conducts research on text linguistics analysis from a post at the Pompeu Fabra University in Barcelona.

In this viewpoint, Teun A. van Dijk provides a theoretical overview of contemporary social scientific perspectives on the news media as an important nexus of social power. He analyzes the ways in which media can manipulate its audience but argues that media consumers can resist manipulation by becoming more familiar with the modes of manipulation. Greater awareness and active engagement on the part of media consumers can help subvert the power dynamics at play.

In the study of mass communication, there has been a continuous debate about the more or less powerful effects of the media on the public.[1] Instead of reviewing these positions and their empirical claims, this chapter examines in more general terms some properties of the social power of the news media. This power is not restricted to the influence of the media on their audiences, but also involves the role of the media within the broader framework of the social, cultural, political, or economic power structures

"Power and the News Media," by Teun A. van Dijk, discourses.org. Reprinted by permission.

of society. In order to focus this discussion better, I limit it to the news media, and in particular to the press, thus ignoring the undoubtedly pivotal role of television and other media genres in mass communication.[2]

The theoretical framework for this inquiry is articulated within the multidisciplinary field of discourse analysis, a domain of study in the humanities and social sciences that systematically examines the structures and functions of text and talk in their social, political, and cultural contexts.[3] Applied to the study of mass communication, this approach claims that in order to understand the role of the news media and their messages, one needs to pay detailed attention to the structures and strategies of such discourses and to the ways these relate to institutional arrangements, on the one hand, and to the audience, on the other hand.[4] For instance, topics or quotation patterns in news reports may reflect modes of access of various news actors or sources to the news media, whereas the content and form of a headline in the press may subtly influence the interpretation and hence the persuasive effects of news reports among the readers. Conversely, if we want to examine what exactly goes on if it is assumed that the media manipulate their readers or viewers, we need to know under what precise conditions, including structural properties of news reports, this might be the case.

Power

A brief conceptual analysis is needed in order to specify what notions of power are involved in such an approach to the role of the news media. I limit this analysis to properties of social or institutional power and ignore the more idiosyncratic dimensions of personal influence, for example, those of individual journalists. Thus, social power here will be summarily defined as a social relation between groups or institutions, involving the control by a (more) powerful group or institution (and its members) of the actions and the minds of (the members) a less powerful group.[5] Such power generally presupposes privileged access to socially valued resources, such as force, wealth, income, knowledge, or status.

Media power is generally symbolic and persuasive, in the sense that the media primarily have the potential to control to some extent the minds of readers or viewers, but not directly their actions.[6] Except in cases of physical, coercive force, the control of action, which is usually the ultimate aim of the exercise of power, is generally indirect, whereas the control of intentions, plans, knowledge, beliefs, or opinions—that is, mental representations that monitor overt activities—is presupposed. Also, given the presence of other sources of information, and because the media usually lack access to the sanctions that other—such as legal or bureaucratic—institutions may apply in cases of noncompliance, mind control by the media can never be complete. On the contrary, psychological and sociological evidence suggests that despite the pervasive symbolic power of the media, the audience will generally retain a minimum of autonomy and independence, and engage more or less actively, instead of purely passively, in the use of the means of mass communication.[7] In other words, whatever the symbolic power of the news media, at least some media users will generally be able to resist such persuasion.

This suggests that mind control by the media should be particularly effective when the media users do not realize the nature or the implications of such control and when they change their minds of their own free will, as when they accept news reports as true or journalistic opinions as legitimate or correct. Such an analysis of social power and its symbolic dimensions requires going beyond a narrow social or political approach to power. It also involves a study of the mental representations, including so-called social cognitions such as attitudes and ideologies, shared by groups of readers or viewers. If we are able to relate more or less explicitly such mental representations, as well as their changes, to properties of news reports, important insights into media power can be gained. Well-known but vague notions such as influence or manipulation may then finally be given a precise meaning.

Within a more critical perspective, many analyses of social power, including those of media power, usually imply references to power abuse—that is, to various forms of the illegitimate or otherwise unacceptable exercise of power, given specific standards, norms, or values. For instance, manipulation as a form of media power enactment is usually evaluated in negative terms, because mediated information is biased or concealed in such a way that the knowledge and beliefs of the audience are changed in a direction that is not necessarily in its best interest. To distinguish legitimate or acceptable power from power abuse, I use the term *dominance* to refer to the latter. Dominance usually involves processes of reproduction that involve strategies aimed at the continued preferential access to social resources and the legitimation of such inequality.

Access

Another important notion in the analysis of (media) power is that of access. It has been shown that power is generally based on special access to valued social resources. This is quite literally also true for access to public discourse, for example, that of the mass media. Thus, controlling the means of mass communication is one of the crucial conditions of social power in contemporary information societies. Indeed, besides economic or other social conditions of power, social groups may be attributed social power by their active or passive access to various forms of public, other influential, or consequential discourse, such as those of the mass media, scholarship, or political and corporate decision making.[8]

Thus, ordinary people usually have active and controlled access only to everyday conversations with family members, friends, or colleagues. Their access to dialogues with officials or professionals, such as lawyers, doctors, or civil servants, is usually constrained in many ways. Although ordinary people may make use of the news media, they generally have no direct influence on news content, nor are they usually the major actors of news reports.

Elite groups or institutions, on the other hand, may be defined by their broader range and scope of patterns of access to public or other important discourses and communicative events. Leading politicians, managers, scholars, or other professionals have more or less controlled access to many different forms of text and talk, such as meetings, reports, press conferences, or press releases. This is especially true for their access to media discourse.[9] Journalists will seek to interview them, ask their opinion, and thus introduce them as major news actors or speakers in news reports. If such elites are able to control these patterns of media access, they are by definition more powerful than the media. On the other hand, those media that are able to control access to elite discourse, in such a way that elites become dependent on them in order to exercise their own power, may in turn play their own role in the power structure. In other words, major news media may themselves be institutions of elite power and dominance, with respect not only to the public at large, but also to other elite institutions.

Access to discourse and communicative events may take many different forms. More powerful social actors may control discourse by setting or selecting time and place, participants, audiences, possible speech acts (such as commands or requests), agendas, topics, choice of language, style, strategies of politeness or deference, and many other properties of text and talk. They thus may essentially determine who may say (or write) what, to whom, about whom, in which way and in what circumstances. It is hereby assumed that social power of a group or institution (and their members) is proportional to the amount of discourse genres and discourse properties they control.

The social power of elite groups and institutions as defined by their preferential access to discourse and communication is effective only if it is further assumed that such discourses are important or influential. Thus, controlling access to the discourses of government sessions, board meetings, or court trials is a manifestation of power because of the consequentiality of such discourse and decision making, that is, because they may seriously affect the lives of many people: The more people affected, the larger the scope of the enactment of discursive power. More specifically, public discourse may affect the minds of many people. Hence, the degree or modes of access to the news media are usually also a measure of the degree of elite power.

Influence and Social Cognition

Special access to the minds of the public does not imply control. Not only does the public have some freedom in participating in the use of media messages, it may also not change its mind along the lines desired by the more powerful. Rejection, disbelief, criticism, or other forms of resistance or challenge may be involved and thus signal modes of counterpower. In other words, *influence* defined as a form of mind control is hardly unproblematic, as is the power of the media and of the elite groups that try to access the public through the media.

In the same way as forms or modes of discourse access may be spelled out, the ways in which the minds of others may indirectly be accessed through text and talk should also be examined. Such an account requires a more explicit insight into the representations and strategies of the social mind. Although I am unable to enter into the technical details of a theory of the mind here as it is being developed in cognitive and social psychology, the very processes of influence involve many different, complex steps and mental (memory) representations, of which I only summarize a few.[10]

Understanding

Readers of a news report first of all need to understand its words, sentences, or other structural properties. This does not only mean that they must know the language and its grammar and lexicon, possibly including rather technical words such as those of modern politics, management, science, or the professions. Users of the media need to know something about the specific organization and functions of news reports in the press, including the functions of headlines, leads, background information, or quotations. Besides such grammatical and textual knowledge, media users need vast amounts of properly organized knowledge of the world. A news report about the Gulf War, for instance, presupposes at least some knowledge about the geography of the Middle East, as well as general knowledge about wars, international politics, earlier historical events, and so on. This means that a lack of education may seriously limit news understanding, as is shown by much empirical research. In other words, powerlessness may involve limited (passive) access to mass-mediated discourse due to a failure (fully) to understand news texts themselves or the events such texts are about.

[...]

Notes

1. The literature on the influence or effects of the mass media is vast. Klapper (1960) is a classic statement. Bradac (1989) and Bryant and Zillmann (1986) are collections of more recent approaches. Early research emphasized the power of the media, a position that gave way to a more skeptical approach to mass media influence when experiments in the 1960s and 1970s often showed little direct effects. Instead, it was then suggested that the media especially have agenda-setting functions: They do not tell people what to think, but what to think about (Iyengar and Kinder 1987; MacKuen and Coombs 1981; McCombs and Shaw 1972). At present there is a tendency to pay attention to significant indirect, overall and ideological influences of the media, for example, in the framework of a critical analysis of the role of the media (see, e.g., Hall, Hobson, Lowe, and Willis 1980; see also later discussion). Besides the earlier quantitative approaches, the question of effect and influence is now also studied in a more qualitative way (see Bruhn Jensen and Jankowski 1991).

2. For the role and influence of television, see, for example, Livingstone (1990), Robinson and Levy (1986), Rowland and Watkins (1984).

3. For different theoretical, analytical, and methodological approaches in discourse analysis, see the contributions and references in van Dijk (1985a). Although there are several introductory studies, none of them cover the whole field of contemporary discourse analysis.

4. This argument is developed in more detail in my book on discourse analytical news theory (van Dijk 1988a, 1988b). These books also give references to other linguistic or textual approaches to news analysis. See also the book by Fowler (1991).

5. The philosophical and social scientific literature on power and related notions is very large. For a conceptual analysis that also informs our approach (although I take a somewhat different perspective and focus on discourse-based, persuasive dimensions of power), see, for example, Lukes (1986); see also Clegg (1989) and Wrong (1979).

6. For the power of the media interpreted as influence on the audience, see the references given in Note 1. For an analysis of the power of the media as an organization, for example, in relation to other elite institutions, see Altheide (1985), Altschull (1984),

Bagdikian (1983), Lichter, Rothman, and Lichter (1990), Paletz and Entman (1981), among many other studies.

7. At present, there is a rather heated debate about this autonomy of the active audience. Some authors within a broader cultural approach emphasize the active uses of the media by the audience (e.g., Liebes and Katz 1990; Morley 1986). Critical approaches to the mass media, however, rather emphasize the manipulative or other influential roles of the media and a more passive public (see, e.g., Schiller 1989). For a brief recent discussion of this debate, see Seaman (1992).

8. There are not many studies that examine the role of access in much detail, either within a general theory of power or more specifically for the news media. For details of this discourse analytical approach to access, see van Dijk (1988a, 1995).

9. Many studies detail, although usually rather informally or anecdotally, this media access power of the elites (see also the references in Note 6). For more systematic and theoretically oriented studies on the routines of news production and the role of elite sources and news actors in newsmaking, see Cans (1979) and Tuchman (1978).

10. For further references and a theoretical background on the cognitive psychology of text comprehension, see van Dijk and Kintsch (1983), who illustrate their theory with an article from *Newsweek*. For specific applications to the study of news, see, for example, Graber (1988), Gunter (1987), Ruhrmann (1989), and van Dijk (1988a). For the role of knowledge in discourse understanding, see Schank and Abelson (1977) and the many other studies that have adopted their notion of script as a mental organization of knowledge.

2

Ethical Issues in Journalism and Media

Leighton Walter Kille

Leighton Walter Kille is a research editor for Journalist's Resource, a web resource operated by Harvard's Shorenstein Center on Media, Politics, and Public Policy, which provides journalists with access to peer-reviewed data and research to assist with their reporting. He was previously on the editorial staff at the Boston Globe.

In this viewpoint, Leighton Walter Kille proposes a specific set of principles for journalists to consider when confronted by ethical issues in the course of their research and reporting work. He argues that it is the responsibility of journalists to uphold standards of truth and keep in mind the public interest when reporting. He also asserts that journalists must strive to make significant information exciting to readers, rather than letting what is sensational guide their coverage.

In 1997 the Carnegie-Knight Task Force, then administered by the Project for Excellence in Journalism, began a national conversation to identify and clarify the principles that underlie journalism. After four years of research, including 20 public forums around the country, a national survey of journalists and more, the group released a Statement of Shared Purpose that identified nine principles. These became the basis for *The Elements of Journalism*, a book by PEJ director Tom Rosenstiel and CCJ chairman and PEJ senior counselor Bill Kovach.

"Committee of Concerned Journalists: The Principles of Journalism," by Leighton Walter Kille, Journalist's Resource, November 26, 2009. https://journalistsresource.org/tip-sheets /foundations/principles-of-journalism. Licensed under CC BY-ND 4.0 International.

Here are those principles, as outlined in the original Statement of Shared Purpose.

Statement of Purpose

The central purpose of journalism is to provide citizens with accurate and reliable information they need to function in a free society. This encompasses myriad roles—helping define community; creating common language and common knowledge; identifying a community's goals, heroes and villains; and pushing people beyond complacency. This purpose also involves other requirements, such as being entertaining, serving as watchdog and offering voice to the voiceless.

Over time journalists have developed nine core principles to meet the task. They comprise what might be described as the theory of journalism:

1. Journalism's First Obligation Is to the Truth

Democracy depends on citizens having reliable, accurate facts put in a meaningful context. Journalism does not pursue truth in an absolute or philosophical sense, but it can—and must—pursue it in a practical sense. This "journalistic truth" is a process that begins with the professional discipline of assembling and verifying facts. Then journalists try to convey a fair and reliable account of their meaning, valid for now, subject to further investigation. Journalists should be as transparent as possible about sources and methods so audiences can make their own assessment of the information. Even in a world of expanding voices, accuracy is the foundation upon which everything else is built—context, interpretation, comment, criticism, analysis and debate. The truth, over time, emerges from this forum. As citizens encounter an ever greater flow of data, they have more need—not less—for identifiable sources dedicated to verifying that information and putting it in context.

2. Its First Loyalty Is to Citizens

While news organizations answer to many constituencies, including advertisers and shareholders, the journalists in those organizations must maintain allegiance to citizens and the larger public interest above any other if they are to provide the news without fear or favor. This commitment to citizens first is the basis of a news organization's credibility, the implied covenant that tells the audience the coverage is not slanted for friends or advertisers. Commitment to citizens also means journalism should present a representative picture of all constituent groups in society. Ignoring certain citizens has the effect of disenfranchising them. The theory underlying the modern news industry has been the belief that credibility builds a broad and loyal audience, and that economic success follows in turn. In that regard, the business people in a news organization also must nurture—not exploit—their allegiance to the audience ahead of other considerations.

3. Its Essence Is a Discipline of Verification

Journalists rely on a professional discipline for verifying information. When the concept of objectivity originally evolved, it did not imply that journalists are free of bias. It called, rather, for a consistent method of testing information—a transparent approach to evidence—precisely so that personal and cultural biases would not undermine the accuracy of their work. The method is objective, not the journalist. Seeking out multiple witnesses, disclosing as much as possible about sources, or asking various sides for comment, all signal such standards. This discipline of verification is what separates journalism from other modes of communication, such as propaganda, fiction or entertainment. But the need for professional method is not always fully recognized or refined. While journalism has developed various techniques for determining facts, for instance, it has done less to develop a system for testing the reliability of journalistic interpretation.

4. Its Practitioners Must Maintain an Independence from Those They Cover

Independence is an underlying requirement of journalism, a cornerstone of its reliability. Independence of spirit and mind, rather than neutrality, is the principle journalists must keep in focus. While editorialists and commentators are not neutral, the source of their credibility is still their accuracy, intellectual fairness and ability to inform—not their devotion to a certain group or outcome. In our independence, however, we must avoid any tendency to stray into arrogance, elitism, isolation or nihilism.

5. It Must Serve as an Independent Monitor of Power

Journalism has an unusual capacity to serve as watchdog over those whose power and position most affect citizens. The Founders recognized this to be a rampart against despotism when they ensured an independent press; courts have affirmed it; citizens rely on it. As journalists, we have an obligation to protect this watchdog freedom by not demeaning it in frivolous use or exploiting it for commercial gain.

6. It Must Provide a Forum for Public Criticism and Compromise

The news media are the common carriers of public discussion, and this responsibility forms a basis for our special privileges. This discussion serves society best when it is informed by facts rather than prejudice and supposition. It also should strive to fairly represent the varied viewpoints and interests in society, and to place them in context rather than highlight only the conflicting fringes of debate. Accuracy and truthfulness require that as framers of the public discussion we not neglect the points of common ground where problem solving occurs.

7. It Must Strive to Make the Significant Interesting and Relevant

Journalism is storytelling with a purpose. It should do more than gather an audience or catalogue the important. For its own survival, it must balance what readers know they want with what they cannot anticipate but need. In short, it must strive to make the significant interesting and relevant. The effectiveness of a piece of journalism is measured both by how much a work engages its audience and enlightens it. This means journalists must continually ask what information has most value to citizens and in what form. While journalism should reach beyond such topics as government and public safety, a journalism overwhelmed by trivia and false significance ultimately engenders a trivial society.

8. It Must Keep the News Comprehensive and Proportional

Keeping news in proportion and not leaving important things out are also cornerstones of truthfulness. Journalism is a form of cartography: it creates a map for citizens to navigate society. Inflating events for sensation, neglecting others, stereotyping or being disproportionately negative all make a less reliable map. The map also should include news of all our communities, not just those with attractive demographics. This is best achieved by newsrooms with a diversity of backgrounds and perspectives. The map is only an analogy; proportion and comprehensiveness are subjective, yet their elusiveness does not lessen their significance.

9. Its Practitioners Must Be Allowed to Exercise Their Personal Conscience

Every journalist must have a personal sense of ethics and responsibility—a moral compass. Each of us must be willing, if fairness and accuracy require, to voice differences with our colleagues, whether in the newsroom or the executive suite. News organizations do well to nurture this independence by encouraging individuals to speak their minds. This stimulates the intellectual diversity necessary to understand and accurately cover an increasingly diverse society. It is this diversity of minds and voices, not just numbers, that matters.

10. Citizens, Too, Have Rights and Responsibilities When It Comes to the News

This principle was added to the original nine principles when *The Elements of Journalism* was revised in April 2007.

3

The End of the Big Media Era

Christopher B. Daly

Christopher B. Daly is a professor of journalism at Boston College. Previously he was a reporter with the Associated Press and the Washington Post.

In this viewpoint, Christopher B. Daly provides an overview of developments in the American media landscape over the course of the last two centuries. He focuses on how the evolution of news media business models affected the way content was delivered to audiences. With the advent of the internet, the role of print news media has become increasingly less essential, and as such news media outlets have had to try harder to grasp onto an audience.

What was it like inside Big Media in the glory days? Here's an account from the journalist John Podhoretz, reminiscing about the 1980s:

> Time Inc., the parent company of *Time,* was flush then. Very, very, very flush. So flush that the first week I was there, the World section had a farewell lunch for a writer who was being sent to Paris to serve as bureau chief . . . at Lutèce, the most expensive restaurant in Manhattan, for 50 people. So flush that if you stayed past 8, you could take a limousine home . . . and take it anywhere, including to the Hamptons if you had weekend plans there. So

"The Decline of Big Media, 1980s–2000s: Key Lessons and Trends," by Christopher B. Daly, Journalist's Resource, August 28, 2013. https://journalistsresource.org/studies /society/news-media/covering-america-journalism-professor-christopher-daly. Licensed under CC BY-ND 4.0 International.

flush that if a writer who lived, say, in suburban Connecticut, stayed late writing his article that week, he could stay in town at a hotel of his choice. So flush that, when I turned in an expense account covering my first month with a $32 charge on it for two books I'd bought for research purposes, my boss closed her office door and told me never to submit a report asking for less than $300 back, because it would make everybody else look bad. So flush that when its editor-in-chief, the late Henry Grunwald, went to visit the facilities of a new publication called *TV Cable Week* that was based in White Plains, a 40-minute drive from the Time Life Building, he arrived by helicopter—and when he grew bored by the tour, he said to his aide, "Get me my helicopter."

In the same period, *Time* was paying its top freelancers in the range of $10 a word (which certainly adds up!). And it was not just *Time* magazine. At the *New York Times,* the journalist R. W. "Johnny" Apple Jr. made a reputation not only for his stylish front-page pieces but also for his outlandish expense accounts, brimming with $400 bottles of wine (followed by expensive brandies) and the best rooms at the best hotels. At the *Washington Post,* the newspaper employed two full-time in-house travel agents just to handle transportation and housing. When reporters needed to go somewhere, they just called the travel desk and let them know. A short while later, a big envelope full of tickets and vouchers would appear. *Have a nice trip.*

Throughout the 1980s and 1990s, the big media grew much bigger, partly on the strength of their growing audiences, but mainly by taking a page from Wall Street's book and engaging in the frenzy of mergers and acquisitions that was then sweeping through the rest of the economy. The media consolidation began in earnest in 1985, placing more and more journalism properties inside giant companies that sometimes had little interest in news. That year, Capital Cities Communication (a company previously unheard of in the news media) bought ABC for $3.5 billion, and General Electric bought RCA and its NBC division for $6.3 billion.

In 1986, CBS underwent a friendly takeover by Laurence Tisch and thus passed out of the effective control of William Paley. In

1989, Time Inc., seeking to become too big to take over, merged with Warner Bros. film studios in a record-setting $14 billion deal. The pace quickened again in the mid-1990s. In 1995, CBS changed hands again, bought by Westinghouse for $5.4 billion. The next year brought the purchase of Cap Cities/ABC by Disney Corp. for some $19 billion. In October 1996, Ted Turner took his Turner Broadcasting System into a merger with Time Warner, Inc., creating the biggest media conglomerate to date and combining the newsgathering companies CNN and *Time* magazine, along with dozens of entertainment properties. In 1999, CBS changed hands yet again when it was bought by Viacom for $37 billion. (It was later spun off and emerged once more as an independent company.) The mentality was simple: grow or die.

Even the giants wanted to get bigger. In 2000, Time Warner merged again, this time teaming up with the Internet phenomenon America Online. Gerald Levin of Time Warner (who never worked as a journalist) was now hitched to Steve Case of AOL (who also never worked as a journalist) in an arrangement that was awkward to begin with and spiraled downhill as AOL began losing money. One casualty of the merger was Ted Turner. When he had brought TBS into the Time Warner fold, Turner solidified his personal fortune, but he was no longer his own boss. Instead, he was given profit targets, just like the heads of other divisions at Time Warner. "For the last four years we were asked to grow 20 percent a year compounded profits for our division. We've done it," Turner said in 2004, but he lamented that the only way to hit those profit targets was to forgo one of his pet projects: hard-hitting documentaries on subjects like the Soviet nuclear program. For a buccaneer with a taste for news, it proved a deal with the devil.

On the day of the AOL–Time Warner merger in 2001, Turner's personal stake in the combined company was worth more than $7 billion. What none of the principals knew was that the stock price was just about at its peak. In less than three years, Turner's stake would shrink to less than $2 billion. As more and more

Internet users discovered how to browse the Web on their own (especially once Google started helping them), they no longer needed to pay AOL a monthly fee to hold their hand. So AOL stopped growing and began imploding financially, threatening the very existence of the company that Henry Luce had founded in 1923. The Time Warner–AOL merger was shaping up as a case of grow *and* die.

Growth, But Not for Journalism

The results of all these corporate mergers and acquisitions was not a net benefit to the practice of journalism. For one thing, most of the deals were, in Wall Street parlance, highly leveraged. That is, the dealmakers used debt rather than cash to buy the properties. As a result, the management was obligated to pay the bankers and bondholders on a relentless schedule. Management issued quarterly profit demands to the heads of divisions for a simple reason: they needed the money. To make matters worse, the stockholders wanted dividends, which also came out of profits, and they wanted to see the value of their shares increase. Under those constraints, big media companies came under tremendous pressure to cut costs and to keep looking for deals that would allow them to borrow even more money to make the company even bigger. The executives who planned and executed these financial maneuvers were not journalists; they were bankers, lawyers, arbitragers, dealmakers. News was not their business; *business* was their business.

At the same time, there were some notable exceptions. Two important ones in the newspaper business were the *New York Times* and the *Washington Post.* Using slightly different techniques, both papers were organized in such a way that the families who owned them exercised effective control over the newspapers at their cores, and both companies were protected from takeovers by outsiders. This meant that the Sulzbergers and the Grahams continued to own (and manage) the two most important daily papers in the country. As long as the money flowed in from circulation and advertising, they could poke a finger in the eye of the federal government, big companies, or almost anyone they thought deserved it. They could maintain costly bureaus in distant places and not have to justify the expense to anyone else. They were not infallible, of course, but they were not subject to corporate overlords, either. The question about both papers at the turn of the century was: How long could it last?

There were other notable exceptions to the corporate takeover of American journalism. Among magazines, several small but important journals of opinion, like the *Nation* or the *New Republic,* had patrons with deep pockets who kept them alive for noneconomic reasons. The *New Yorker* had survived its first few years courtesy of the largesse of Raoul Fleischmann. Then, for decades, it was immensely profitable, right up until 1967, when the number of advertising pages began to drop precipitously. Then followed years of turmoil and turnover, including the sale of the magazine by the Fleischmann family to the privately held Advance Publications, owned by S. I. Newhouse. The *New Yorker* lost money for eighteen years until it was folded into Condé Nast (a division of Advance Publications) in 1999, and it became modestly profitable again under editor David Remnick while continuing to win prizes and astound readers.

Another major exception to the Wall Street model was National Public Radio, which flourished during these years as a nonprofit. With a growing budget, NPR strengthened its newsgathering capacity, both at home and abroad, and emerged as a major source of news and commentary. The government's contribution to its budget continued to shrink, as NPR came to rely more and more on sponsors and on "listeners like you." By 2010 the biggest single source was the voluntary donations from the audience. In addition, another major source of news in America was that venerable cooperative the Associated Press, which supplied a vast amount of hard news (along with sports and business reporting, as well as photos and video) to nearly all of the nation's news outlets. It remained nonprofit as well.

The most powerful trend in the news business in the late twentieth century was the reorganization of most news outlets into parts of large, publicly traded corporations, often without the ultimate consumers even noticing. In the newspaper field, chains like Gannett, Knight-Ridder, and McClatchy—hardly household names to most readers—gobbled up formerly independent papers. In radio, Clear Channel bought its one thousandth radio station in 2000. Television ownership actually expanded a bit with the arrival of Fox News (a division of News Corp.), but the industry remained one of limited sellers and enormous barriers to entry. The magazine business, too, followed a similar pattern, except that most of the biggest players—Advance Publications (which owns Fairchild Publications as well as the Condé Nast group) and Hearst Corporation—were both privately held companies.

It might be asked: So what? What difference does it make if the news business is, like most of the rest of the economy, in the hands of big corporations? Isn't the publicly traded corporation the engine that drives the US economy, giving it the dynamism that makes it the envy of the world? It's a fair question. In the history of the news business, the form of ownership has always mattered, from the colonial print shop through the industrial, family-owned era, to the corporate phase. In the transformation of the news business into a corporate form and then into a conglomerate form, the changes have not been neutral for journalism. The older forms were not perfect—far from it, as the record indicates. But the transformation of traditional media in the late twentieth century also came at a high cost in several respects.

One problem was the drive toward monopoly—or if not monopoly, then what economists call "concentration." As the number of different owners in any industry shrinks, that industry changes. The survivors face less competition, and they often find it easier as a result to raise prices. If there is a single survivor in the field, then the winner can take all. In the news business, this pattern threatens the very existence of diverse, and local, points of view. Clear Channel replaced more than one thousand individual owners, with different aspirations, different ideas about their civic roles, and different ideologies. The number of US cities with healthy, competing daily newspapers, once in the hundreds, fell to about a dozen. By the year 2000, in American cities that had a daily newspaper, 99 percent had only one management in town. The fifteen biggest newspaper chains account for more than half the nation's total circulation. In all, there were about 1,500 daily newspapers remaining in America. Of those, only about 350 were independently owned, and most of those were very small. The whole industry was heading in a direction that was at odds with the journalistic values of independence, localism, and competition.

The Problem with Big

Housing news operations inside such huge conglomerates gave rise to problems. One was the ethical quandary known as conflict of interest. For decades, journalists sought to be independent so that readers and viewers could trust that they were getting the straight dope—about government, about business, even about sports. The idea was that journalists should be able to tell it like it is, without worrying about who benefits or suffers from what their reporting turns up. Independence was the professional ideal. But inside conglomerates, no news operation could be even close to independent. In a notorious example, ABC investigative reporter Brian Ross came across a juicy story. Officials at Disneyworld in Orlando were so hard-pressed to find security guards that they were hiring convicted sex offenders to look after the safety of children visiting the theme park. But his superiors at ABC News decided to sit on the story for fear of offending their own superiors at Disney corporate headquarters. (Those ABC execs had not actually been threatened or told what to do; they were just anticipating the reaction.) All of the paychecks at ABC News come from Disney Corp., so why bite the hand that feeds them?

If ABC had still been independent, Ross could have reported his findings and let the chips fall where they may.

Even when there is no pressure (or anticipation of pressure), the ethical problem persists inside big conglomerates. The problem that cannot be eliminated is the *appearance* of a conflict of interest, which can be just as damaging to an institution's credibility as an actual conflict. Under parent company GE, for example, every reporter and every editor at NBC News knew that GE made heavy industrial products like jet engines and wind turbines. How aggressive could they have been in looking into problems in those industries? And even if they were professionally aggressive in pursuit of news in those fields, some number of members of the audience were surely aware that NBC's parent company made those products and would, as a result, have remained suspicious. Or to take another example: the Washington Post company owns not only the *Washington Post* newspaper but also Kaplan, Inc., which coaches students on how to pass standardized tests. How aggressive can *Post* reporters be in evaluating the test-prep business? And even if they do their best, why should readers believe anything they say about Kaplan? Especially since the test-coaching division surpassed the newspaper as the biggest producer of revenue for the parent company. No corporation that includes news and non-news divisions can entirely escape the question of apparent (or structural) conflicts of interest. The problem is inherent in the model.

There are other problems with conglomerate news. While the news divisions may enjoy a measure of independence and First Amendment protections, the likelihood is that some other part of the company is regulated by one or more government agencies. All broadcasters, for example, are regulated by the FCC. Moreover, if the parent company is big enough, there is a likelihood that it sells products or services to the federal or state governments. In that case, how aggressively can the news division be expected to carry out its traditional watchdog role?

In fact, most large corporations are inherently unsuited to the practice of journalism. There is an innate caution that is part of the DNA of any large corporation. Large corporations employ large numbers of people—including legions of attorneys, consultants, accountants, and executives (the people known as "the suits")—who all have perfectly sane and logical reasons for *not* doing a particular investigation, satire, or routine news story. It is not part of their makeup to go around antagonizing other powerful institutions. Why would a division of GE want to pick a fight with the Pentagon? Why would a company like Westinghouse, which hopes to sell products to the largest possible number of customers worldwide, want one of its divisions, CBS, to investigate an institution like the Catholic Church, or even the Mafia? As a business matter, such an investigation is suicide. But as a journalistic matter, it is essential.

Bad News on the Doorstep

When trouble came, it came fast. Newspapers that measured their lives in centuries, magazines that rounded their circulations to the nearest million, networks that had annual revenues in the billions, all of them thinking that they were on a never-ending upswell of money, power, and sway—all of them went over the cliff together. At the very end of the twentieth century, in December 1999, the value of a share of stock in Time Warner, Inc., one of the mightiest of the Big Five media conglomerates, hit its all-time high: $254 a share. Ten years later it was trading at about $25 a share. In a decade, 90 percent of the value of the company had vaporized. It was not an isolated case.

No sooner had the new millennium arrived than gloom settled over most traditional news media. All of a sudden, revenues were flat or down. Budgets were tighter. Part of the problem was the dot-com economic bust, which was causing the high-flying computer-related companies to slash or eliminate their advertising budgets. Those companies also stopped their initial public offerings of stock, so there were no more of those full-page IPO announcements in the business press. Then came September 11, and suddenly the news mattered again. Americans flipped on their radios and TVs and kept them on. The day after and the day after that, newsstands were sold out of papers. Maybe the news was important after all. Then came the economic aftershock, a mini-recession that made everything even worse. But, the thinking went, maybe this was just temporary and things would turn around. Still, the fact was that the money just wasn't there. Cuts would have to be made. First came the easy things: expense accounts, part-timers, freelancers, stringers. But those didn't add up to much. Then came bigger cuts: foreign bureaus, then domestic bureaus, even the Washington bureau. At television news divisions, at the big news-oriented magazines, and at big newspapers, the story was the same.

The economy recovered, but not the news business. By 2004–5 there was a steady drumbeat of cuts, contraction, and worry. Now the cuts were reaching into the heart of most operations, into the newsroom itself. News managers tried to shrink their budgets by offering "buyouts"—in effect, a severance package to pay senior staffers (the ones who were making top pay and who had earned the longest vacations) to go away. When that didn't solve the problem, the next step was out-and-out layoffs. Many a newsroom became the scene of tearful goodbyes, as security guards watched reporters and editors box up a career's worth of mementos and junk, then escorted them out of the building. Still, things got worse. In 2008–9 the news was about bankruptcies—the Tribune Company, Philadelphia Media, the Sun-Times Company. Five major newspaper companies filed for bankruptcy between December 2008 and March 2009 and kept publishing while they sought to reorganize their debts. A few newspapers took the ultimate step and closed up shop altogether, or they abandoned print and became available only online. The wolf was not just through the door, it was also devouring institutions that had been decades, even centuries in the making.

The High Price of Fixed Costs

The most endangered of the "legacy" media was also the oldest: the daily newspaper. The problems besetting the typical newspaper by the end of the first decade of the 21st century were many and serious. One was a cost structure that was in part the result of having been in business so long. Like the Big Three automakers, which were also facing extinction at the same time, most large newspapers had enormous "fixed costs." That is, they were committed to spending a certain large amount of money every day that they did business. Among newspapers at this time, the first fixed cost a publisher faced was the debt incurred in growing to the size of a chain or conglomerate. Just paying the interest on the debt could be crushing. Then there were pensions—legal obligations to keep paying people who hadn't worked at the paper for years or decades, people hired before the current executives were even born. Those were costs that startups, like all those brand-new news sites and aggregators on the Web, did not face. Plus there were health care costs, and the price of buying health insurance was going through the roof. On top of that there was the payroll, and at most big newspapers that meant union contracts—covering pressmen, drivers, photographers, reporters, you name it—that spelled out how much everyone had to be paid, including overtime in a lot of jobs, and all the vacation, sick leave, and other benefits dreamed up in the good times. To make matters worse, a newspaper company operates what is, in effect, a manufacturing plant. Every day it needs large amounts of raw materials. Tons of paper and buckets of ink have to be fed into enormous presses. Out the other end come hundreds of thousands of objects that have to be placed on a fleet of waiting trucks (no matter how high the price of diesel fuel) and hauled through the crowded streets of the home city, through every suburb round about, and hundreds of miles away to the far reaches of the circulation area. The next day, it all has to happen again.

That kind of operation, with its vast overhead, is utterly dependent on seeing a large and steady stream of revenue coming in to support it all. But in recent years, while most of the costs remained fixed, the revenue went steadily downward. Department stores, once the mainstay of big-city papers, with their full-page ads spreading over multiple pages several days a week, consolidated and stopped competing against one another. In the process, they cut way back on their newspaper advertising. In the classified ad department, long an important profit center at most papers, the phones stopped ringing. The people who needed to sell stuff and the people looking to buy stuff met up on Craigslist or eBay or some other online site and didn't need the newspaper any more. There went another major source of revenue. Finally, young people mostly stopped reading newspapers—or they stopped reading the *print* version. Survey after survey showed publishers that the print audience was shrinking and aging. The people in nursing homes were not the demographic that was going to keep the business afloat. But it seemed that almost everyone else was flocking to the Web, where they could get news for free, and letting their subscriptions expire. There went another big revenue source.

Another problem besetting newspapers (and, to a great extent, magazines and television news as well) was even more existential. When seen against the backdrop of the Internet, one fact about newspapers becomes painfully obvious: a newspaper is a fixed bundle of coverage that is good but ultimately second rate. Offering readers no choice, a newspaper presents coverage of a set matrix of topics: politics, crime, business, sports, arts, and something called lifestyle. In each case, though, people who really know or care about those fields understand that they are not going to find the absolute best, most detailed, most passionate coverage of their favorite topic in a daily newspaper. They know that the best coverage will be in some niche on the Web where obsessive amateurs or professional experts gather. And with the coming of the Web, the absolute best coverage is available to everyone, everywhere, all the time, for free. In politics, for example, readers can find pretty good coverage in the *Times* or *Newsweek*. But if they really live and breathe politics, they will want it faster and at a much higher level of granularity, so they will log on to a site like Politico or Real Clear Politics instead and get what they are looking for. The same is true for business, sports, even crosswords and recipes. Thus the question arises: What is the remaining value of reading merely pretty good coverage (and paying for it) when readers can unbundle the newspaper, go online, and plunge into first-rate coverage, written by real aficionados and provided at a price of zero?

One way to understand the decline of the newspaper is to ask the ultimate question: If newspapers did not exist, would it make any sense to invent them?

4

The Relationship Between Conservative Media and Politics in America

Jackie Calmes

Jackie Calmes is the White House editor for the Los Angeles Times. *Previously she was a correspondent at the* Wall Street Journal *and the* New York Times. *In 2005, she received the Gerald R. Ford Journalism Prize for Reporting on the Presidency.*

Jackie Calmes looks at the influence of conservative journalists and media organizations on the policy platform of the Republican Party, with an emphasis on the period of time immediately following the 2012 presidential election. She assesses the extent to which conservative media succeeds at shaping political elections and policy. The viewpoint also explores how social media has allowed the more radical conservative voices to find an audience and have a greater impact on political discourse.

Republicans should still have been celebrating in late January 2015. Only weeks earlier they had opened the 114th Congress with a Senate majority for the first time in eight years, as well as a fattened majority in the House, where they had ruled since 2011— full control of the legislative branch for the first time in Barack Obama's presidency. Yet in reality, Republicans were out of control. They only had themselves to blame, and many did. So unhappy

"Conservative Media's Influence on the Republican Party," by Jackie Calmes, Shorenstein Center, July 27, 2015. https://shorensteincenter.org/conservative-media-influence-on -republican-party-jackie-calmes. Licensed under CC BY-ND 3.0 Unported.

was Representative Charlie Dent, a six-term Pennsylvanian and one of the few surviving Republican moderates, he emerged from a private party caucus in January to share with reporters waiting outside the complaint he had made to colleagues behind closed doors: "Week one, we had a speaker election that did not go as well as a lot of us would have liked. Week two, we got into a big fight over deporting children, something that a lot of us didn't want to have a discussion about. Week three, we are now talking about rape and incest and reportable rapes and incest for minors," Dent said. "I just can't wait for week four."[1]

Indeed, the coming weeks only got worse. That owed to a February showdown with President Obama over immigration policy that Republican leaders had teed up back in December, during a lame-duck Congress, when their immediate concern was getting their militant members out of town for the holidays without provoking another government shutdown. But they knew then that they were merely postponing the inevitable, a battle doomed to fail at the opening of the new, Republican-led Congress. Much like Republicans' politically disastrous ploy in the fall of 2013, when they shuttered the government to try to force Obama to support repeal of his signature domestic achievement, the Affordable Care Act, this early 2015 clash with the president also turned on an empty threat—Republicans implausibly vowed to withhold money for homeland security programs, even as terrorist acts filled the news, unless Obama agreed to reverse his recent executive actions on immigration and deport millions of young people brought to the country illegally as children, and their parents, too. Come January 2015 House Speaker John A. Boehner and Senate Majority Leader Mitch McConnell gamely led the charge. It predictably backfired and by March the unhappy duo engineered the retreat they had known would have to come. Congress approved a "clean" bill funding homeland security, without any language restricting the administration on immigration.

It was a humiliating debut for a party that had promised in the 2014 midterm elections that Republicans would show the nation how well they could govern, if only voters would put them completely in charge of Congress. Considering that the humiliation was self-inflicted (Did anyone really believe McConnell, one of Congress's wiliest players, would have scripted this chaotic curtain-raiser?), no drama could have better demonstrated that the leaders of the Republican Party do not fully control its agenda. By spring, Congress did pass a series of significant measures—addressing terrorism insurance, human trafficking and veterans' suicides, for instance, and fixing a longtime policy headache involving Medicare reimbursements to doctors. But Democrats' cooperation had helped, and no one interpreted those achievements as a sign that Republicans would be able to perform the bigger, essential governing tasks that loomed, of passing annual appropriations bills and raising the nation's debt limit, without the messy intraparty ruptures and brinkmanship of recent years.[2]

That other forces were shaping Republicans' agenda was likewise evident on a parallel track, as their party began the long process of picking a 2016 presidential nominee. Here, too, the immigration issue was front-and-center, and not in the way that the Republican leadership had called for in its unsparing autopsy of the party's 2012 election losses. That earlier analysis, commissioned by the chairman of the Republican National Committee, Reince Priebus, had called for "positive solutions on immigration" and less divisive rhetoric; nominee Mitt Romney, who had called on undocumented immigrants to "self-deport," had received just 27 percent of the votes from an expanding Latino electorate, when at least 40 percent was considered essential for victory—a threshold that will rise as the Latino voting population does. "If Hispanic Americans hear that the GOP doesn't want them in the United States, they won't pay attention to our next sentence," the party study said. "It doesn't matter what we say about education, jobs or the economy."[3]

Two years later, Republicans' positions and rhetoric on immigration could not be more contrary to that advice. While Jeb Bush, the Republican establishment's favorite for 2016 and a

Spanish-speaking former governor of Florida, has just the sort of record that party elders had in mind—long favoring a legal path to citizenship for an estimated 11 million undocumented residents—he is widely perceived as a weakened, even fatally flawed candidate for the nomination because of it. Similarly, another contender who had been hailed as a new-generation star, Florida's Senator Marco Rubio, by 2015 was being all but written off by many conservative media figures and activists for having been part of a bipartisan "Gang of Eight" in the Senate that in 2013 won overwhelming passage of a comprehensive immigration bill, which then died in the Republican-led House of willful neglect.

Worse for Bush, he also is on the wrong side of what has become another litmus test in Republicans' presidential race: the so-called Common Core education standards. Conceived some years ago as a bipartisan initiative of the nation's governors, Common Core by 2013 had been redefined by hardline conservatives in media and activist groups as an attempted federal takeover of public school classrooms. So when the 2016 field began taking shape, once-supportive Republicans including Bobby Jindal, Mike Huckabee and Chris Christie reversed themselves. Bush did not, but by this year he was neither advertising his support nor using the words "Common Core."

If leaders of the Republican Party are not setting its agenda, who is?

As many of them concede, it is conservative media—not just talk-show celebrities Rush Limbaugh, Sean Hannity, Mark Levin and Laura Ingraham, but also lesser-known talkers like Steve Deace, and an expanding web of "news" sites and social media outlets with financial and ideological alliances with far-right anti-government, anti-establishment groups like Heritage Action, Americans for Prosperity, Club for Growth and FreedomWorks. Once allied with but now increasingly hostile to the Republican hierarchy, conservative media is shaping the party's agenda in ways that are impeding Republicans' ability to govern and to win presidential elections. "These people, practically speaking, are preventing the Republican Party from governing, which means they're really preventing it from becoming a presidential party as well," said Geoffrey Kabaservice, author of *Rule and Ruin: The Downfall of Moderation and the Destruction of the Republican Party, from Eisenhower to the Tea Party*, and himself a Republican.[4]

And who is Steve Deace? The baby-faced 41-year-old Deace (pronounced Dace) is a college dropout, self-described one-time loser, former part-time sports writer and born-again Christian who one day unexpectedly found himself with a radio show in Iowa, home of the first-in-the-nation contest for aspiring presidential nominees. Nine years later, he is nationally syndicated from Des Moines and a prolific columnist and social media presence with tens of thousands of followers. As such, the entrepreneurial Deace exemplifies the otherwise obscure and deeply conservative new-media figures who, collectively, often call the shots in the Republican Party, by both provoking and amplifying the party's conservative activists and their hardline positions. His motto is "Fear God. Tell the Truth. Make Money."

Twenty years ago, former radio shock-jock Rush Limbaugh was mostly alone, though soon to be joined by Roger Ailes and Rupert Murdoch's Fox News Channel in playing to conservative audiences and validating their biases. Since then—to an extent unimagined as recently as Barack Obama's election—the combination of the Internet and social media, broadcast deregulation and technological advances like live-streaming and on-demand audio and video "products" have allowed these new voices and scribblers to proliferate, empowering figures who boast of being more conservative than Fox and "El Rushbo" to shape Republican politics.

"It's not just talk radio, but the blogosphere, the Internet—they're all intertwined now. You've got this constant chorus of skepticism about anything the quote-unquote establishment does," said a longtime former top aide to House Republican leaders, Dave Schnittger. And, he said, the chorus is loudest in opposition to those actions that are fundamental to governing: meeting basic fiscal deadlines for funding the government and allowing it to borrow. "Those are the things that leaders have to get done as part of governing," the Republican said, "as much as conservative media may hate it."[5]

Said another Republican, who has worked in the top ranks of congressional and presidential politics, but, like some others, asked to remain unidentified lest he provoke the far-right messengers against his current boss: "It's so easy these days to go out there and become an Internet celebrity by saying some things, and who cares if it's true or makes any sense. It's a new frontier: How far to the right can you get? And there's no incentive to ever really bother with reality." Or to compromise: "There's no money, ratings or clicks in everyone going along to get along."

Asked whether he could offer examples of legislative outcomes affected by conservative media, this Republican all but snapped, "Sure. All of 'em." Does he worry more broadly then about the small-d democratic process? "Yeah, absolutely. Because the loudest voices drown out the sensible ones and there's no real space to have serious discussions."[6]

"One of the realities here is that these people have always existed," said Norman J. Ornstein, a political scientist at the center-right American Enterprise Institute and co-author with Thomas E. Mann of the book *It's Even Worse Than It Looks*, about what the authors see as the radicalization of the Republican Party. "But they were at the fringes, the John Birch Society types. Now, because of social media and because you have a culture of extremism that is not culled out more generally, they can move into the mainstream and actually hijack a major party. And that's what's going on here."[7]

Those in the maligned Republican Party establishment—including many who not so long ago were themselves proud troublemakers for the conservative cause, and who are conservative still by any rational measure—are left to wonder whether the Republican Party is capable of governing. "I would say there is a serious question of whether or not it's a governing party," said Vin Weber, a Republican strategist and former congressman from

Minnesota, who in the 1980s was, along with Newt Gingrich, a leader of right-wing, anti-establishment rebels in the House.[8] As he and congressional leaders fear, this winter's intraparty collision over homeland-security spending and immigration will look trifling compared to likely fights ahead in 2015 over must-pass spending bills and increasing the debt limit again to avert default.

Establishment Republicans say they aspire to push their party closer to society's political center—on immigration, gay rights, climate change and more—much as Democrats slowly moderated from a leftist party in the 1970s to a left-of-center one by the Clinton era, or as Britain's Labor Party similarly shifted under Tony Blair in the late 1990s. In that, these Republicans agree with Mann and Ornstein, who wrote in a 2013 afterword to their book: "After losing five of six presidential elections between 1968 and 1988, Democrats (thanks in large part to the Democratic Leadership Council and Bill Clinton) made a striking adjustment that put them in a position to nominate credible presidential candidates, develop center-left policies responsive to the interests of a majority of voters, and govern in a less ideological, more pragmatic, problem-solving mode. Nothing would contribute more to strengthening American democracy than Republicans going through that same experience."[9]

Yet even though it is now Republicans who have lost the popular vote for president in five of the last six elections, party leaders lament that Democrats' late 20th century model for moderating is inoperative for Republicans in this 21st century Internet age. The problem, as they see it: Conservative media, having helped push the party so far to the anti-government, anti-compromise ideological right, attacks Republican leaders for taking the smallest step toward the moderate middle. "In the late '80s and early '90s, Democrats weren't dealing with a media that has become the way the conservative media has become," which is "much more powerful than John Boehner and Mitch McConnell," said Matthew Dowd, a strategist in George W. Bush's campaigns. Democratic leaders "didn't have to deal with a quote-unquote liberal media out there that was going to confront them every time they took a turn."[10]

"If you stray the slightest from the far right," said former Senate Majority Leader Trent Lott, who continues to advise Republican congressional leaders, "you get hit by the conservative media."[11] David Price, a longtime Democratic congressman from North Carolina and a former political science professor, said, "One of the generalizations we all grew up with in political science is how candidates have to tend to the middle—that's where the votes are. Republicans have changed that."[12] Weber, the former Republican congressman, complained that while elected representatives should reflect the views of their constituents, "the problem you have in the Republican Party is that people are adjusting farther than they really need to"—to avoid a primary challenge.[13]

Conservative media indeed draws much of its power, Republicans say, from incumbents' fear of a primary challenge. Not surprisingly, talk-show hosts and conservative pundits stoke that fear by inviting challengers to run against incumbents deemed too quick to compromise, and then encourage support for them, including financially. Some Republicans say that dynamic—incumbents' fear, media's threat—was intensified in last year's midterm elections despite the party's overall triumphs. Among the few Republican losers was a big one: Eric Cantor, the House majority leader. He had been widely seen as heir apparent to Boehner, and conservatives' choice—until he began arguing that Republicans should support legal status for so-called Dreamers, young people brought to this country illegally as children. Cantor thereby revived many conservatives' suspicions about whether he really was one of them.

Laura Ingraham, the nationally syndicated talk-show host and a vehement foe of immigration reforms, decided to promote Cantor's dark-horse rival in Virginia's Republican primary, Dave Brat, and then was called a giant-killer when Brat unexpectedly won. While Republicans quibble over how much Ingraham actually had to do with the result—Cantor had, they agree, neglected his

Richmond-area district as his national prominence grew—his defeat left many congressional incumbents further cowed by the power of conservative media, and hardened against immigration. "Immigration reform, any hope of it, just basically died," said a senior Senate aide.[14] That solidifying of opposition contributed to Republicans' miscalculations in December's lame-duck session, when they made funding for homeland security contingent on Obama repealing his immigration policies. As further evidence of the Cantor fallout, one House Republican leader recalled in an interview how many Virginia Republicans had defied Boehner in March when he put to a vote a bill to fund homeland security programs for three more weeks to buy time for negotiations with Democrats on immigration. And not just Virginians, the leader said: "Guys that you would normally expect to be okay you could see responding to the political pressure. They saw the immigration issue as a major issue in Eric's defeat."[15] Not for the first or last time, the speaker lost due to party defections.

As for those in the widening world of conservative media, for all of their complaints about the establishment, they are only too happy to acknowledge their influence in shaping the political agenda. "I don't think conservative media is shaping it as much as it would like to, but it's shaping it more than Washington would like it to," said Deace. "I don't think it's moving fast enough for conservatives like myself, but it is clearly dragging the Republicans along, kicking and screaming."[16]

Setting the agenda, however, is not the same as winning, whether in the congressional or presidential arenas. Conservative media, and the conservative activists the media gives voice to, often do not win: Witness the retreat on the homeland security and immigration fight this year, the failed 2013 government shutdown, or Romney's nomination over more conservative rivals in 2012. Or consider House Republicans' futile 50-plus attempts to repeal all or part of Obama's health-insurance law, and without offering any alternative plan, given the opposition among conservative media and activists to any role for the federal government.

Yet those in conservative media, whether in print, online, or radio and TV broadcasting, invariably see these fights as a win-win: They and their audiences repeatedly get to set the agenda, to provoke a confrontation in defense of what they see as conservative principles. And when the fight fails—well, that is Republican leaders' fault for not fighting hard enough. Conservative media can always find a like-minded politician—say, senator and presidential candidate Ted Cruz—to say so. And with each loss or retreat, conservative media and its readers, viewers and listeners are only further enraged at the Republican establishment. That anger was behind the divisive first act of the new Republican Congress: House conservatives' attempt to oust Boehner as speaker.

Similarly, conservative media figures see the process of picking presidential nominees as a win-win. Establishment Republicans are quick to point out, as two did in interviews in identical terms, "Their track record is not very good."[17] But while those in conservative media generally have not picked recent Republican nominees, they have defined the terms of debate. By backing the most conservative contenders and enforcing litmus tests, they have forced the ultimate nominee further right—weakening Romney and, before him, Senator John McCain among swing voters in the general election. Yet when the nominee loses, that is the fault of his campaign and the national party, in conservative media's telling.

In 2008 and 2012, conservative media did not coalesce around a single candidate. In 2008, many in the media ultimately supported Romney in an unsuccessful bid to block McCain after their first choices, like former minister and Arkansas governor Huckabee, foundered. But four years later, with several ideological conservatives in the running, most in conservative media opposed Romney as a flip-flopping moderate-in-disguise—a dread RINO, Republican In Name Only. Romney's call for illegal immigrants to "self-deport," so damaging in the end, was his way of getting to the right of rivals, chiefly Texas Governor Rick Perry, and playing to conservative media—and through them to conservative voters during the primaries.

Weber, the former insurgent congressman turned

establishment leader, said of conservative media, "What's bad from the 2012 campaign is not that they won, but that they set the agenda. What difference did it make to the Republican Party to have Romney defeat Rick Santorum if Romney's going to embrace an agenda to the right of Rick Santorum?"[18] More generally, said a Republican who asked to remain unidentified, "There's not a platform in the Laura Ingraham-Sean Hannity wing of conservatism. There's nothing that you can take to the country and hope to win the presidency on that they believe in. I mean, anti-immigration, don't hesitate to shut down the government, repeal Obamacare, no new taxes—that's not a governing platform. That will rally 40 percent of the population."[19]

That is not, of course, how those in conservative media see it. Especially in talk radio, they argue—as their media predecessors did in the first decades after World War II—that Republicans win the White House when their message and their messenger are truly conservative, "a choice, not an echo" of Democrats, as Phyllis Schlafly famously wrote in 1964. To this day, conservatives' certainty of that is undimmed by the fact that in the year of Schlafly's book, right wing media and activists finally had prevailed in seeing their choice, Barry Goldwater, nominated, only to have him lose in a landslide and drag other Republicans with him. That defeat, conservative media insisted at the time, was the failure of the party establishment, which did not rally behind Goldwater and in some cases joined the liberal media and Democrats in labeling him an extremist. Looking toward 2016, once again the search for a true conservative animates the Republican right, but with an increased intensity that reflects the proliferation and combativeness of conservative media. As in recent quadrennials, conservative media is not united behind a candidate to favor, only the one to oppose: Jeb Bush. In February the *Washington Post* had a story headlined "Jeb Bush has a serious talk radio problem,"[20] followed in March by a *Politico* story entitled "Jeb's Talk Radio Problem."[21] By all accounts, and as Bush himself has suggested, his candidacy will test whether a

Republican can run without pandering to conservative media, and with mainly the November electorate in mind.

[…]

Endnotes

[1] Lauren Fox and Daniel Newhauser, "GOP Leaders Pull Abortion Bill After Revolt By Women, Moderates," *The National Journal*, 21 January 2015, http://www.theatlantic.com/politics/archive/2015/01/gop-leaders-pull-abortionbill- after-revolt-by-women-moderates/446133/.

[2] Carl Hulse, "Parties Coming to More Agreement (Just Not on Who Deserves Credit)," *The New York Times*, May 4, 2015, http://www.nytimes.com/2015/05/05/us/politics/parties-are-agreeing-more-justnot- on-the-reason.html.

[3] Henry Barbour et al., "The Growth and Opportunity Project," the Republican National Committee (2013): 15-16, http://goproject.gop.com/rnc_growth_opportunity_book_2013.pdf.

[4] Geoffrey Kabaservice, interview with author, March 4, 2015.

[5] David Schnittger, interview with author, February 19, 2015.

[6] Republican adviser, interview with author, February 6, 2015.

[7] Norman J. Ornstein, interview with author, December 3, 2014.

[8] Vin Weber, interview with author, February 5, 2015.

[9] Norman J. Ornstein and Thomas E. Mann, 2013 afterward to *It's Even Worse Than It Looks—How the American Constitutional System Collided with the New Politics of Extremism* (New York: Basic Books, 2012).

[10] Matthew Dowd, interview with author, January 7, 2015.

[11] Trent Lott, interview with author, February 24, 2015.

[12] David Price, interview with author, March 18, 2015.

[13] Vin Weber.

[14] Senate aide, interview with author, March 23, 2015.

[15] House Republican leadership member, interview with author, March 2015.

[16] Steve Deace, interview with the author, March 2, 2015.

[17] Two Republican strategists, interviews with author, February 2015.

[18] Vin Weber.

[19] Republican, interview with author, February 2015.

[20] Jose A. DelReal, "Jeb Bush Has a Serious Talk Radio Problem," *The Washington Post*, February 2, 2015, http://www.washingtonpost.com/blogs/post-politics/wp/2015/02/02/jeb-bush-has-a-serious-talk-radio-problem/.

[21] Michael Kruse, "Jeb's Talk Radio Problem," *Politico*, March 22, 2015, http://www.politico.com/magazine/story/2015/03/jeb-bush-rush-limbaugh-talk-radio-116283.html#.VUqD96bQm6M.

5

News, Journalism, and Comedy

Rachel Joy Larris

Rachel Joy Larris holds a master of arts degree in communication, culture, and technology from the Georgetown University Graduate School of Arts and Sciences.

Rachel Joy Larris examines the "new hybrid of political and entertainment programming" represented by television shows like The Daily Show with Jon Stewart *and* Real Time with Bill Maher. *She outlines some of the key social and political issues raised by this new media form, such as the decreased influence of news media in shaping political opinions and the impact this has on democracy.*

> "A lot of television viewers—more, quite frankly, than I am comfortable with—get their news from [...] *The Daily Show.*"
>
> — *Ted Koppel to Jon Stewart, Nightline, July 28, 2004*

For decades now, the youngest segment of the American public has been losing interest in the news. Surveys of media usage for people ages 18 to 29 show they consume traditional news media—newspapers and network news programs—at much lower rates then either their parents or grandparents (Pew Research Center 2000, Pew Research Center 2004). This has led to concerns voiced by political scholars and politicians alike as to where this segment of society is getting their news and where they will get their news when they are older. The youngest generation's general disinterest

"The Daily Show Effect: Humor, News, Knowledge and Viewers," by Rachel Joy Larris, Georgetown University Library, May 2, 2005. Reprinted by permission.

in political news from an early age lends itself to the belief that this is the cause for decreasing levels of voting across generations because, as the youngest age, they do not gain an interest in news or politics (Patterson 2002). This disinterest creates patterns of non-traditional news followers who do not watch the nightly news and do not read newspapers. To many, this is a cause for concern. A view of democracy, dating back to the Progressive era, cites that the cornerstone of American democracy presupposes that there is an informed citizenry. Even our country's founding forefathers waxed eloquent about the role of newspapers, i.e. news, in their society. An uninformed citizen is one who cannot guide the actions of their government. In any case those who do not follow the news regularly are far less likely to vote (Patterson 2002).

When this country was founded there existed only one news format: print, specifically in the form of newspapers and pamphlets. As technology developed and evolved so have news media forums changed, grown, and expanded. Broadcasting, beginning with radio frequencies, then later network television and cable television, all became forums for news. However, as the news media have expanded they have also fractured into thousands of different audiences. Whereas a generation ago Americans' primary sources of news were limited to the daily 8 newspaper and the local and national evening news broadcasts on one of the three networks, today there is a plethora of news source choices. The burgeoning "new media" has been best defined by Richard Davis and Diana Owen as "mass communication forms with primarily nonpolitical origins that have acquired political roles" (Davis and Owen 1998, 7).

Among these new forms is the late-night talk show. The late-night talk show generally has both comedic and interview components to it. In 2004, the Pew Research Center for People and the Press released a survey containing a widely reported fact that 21% of people ages 18 to 29 reported they regularly learned some news about political candidates or the 2004 presidential campaign from "comedy TV shows" and 13% reported the same of "late-night TV shows" (Pew Research Center 2004). This survey finding produced a flurry of hand-wringing from news pundits, as if the survey respondents said they were getting all of their daily news from the backs of cereal boxes. Some even misunderstood the survey findings, assuming they meant that respondents were *primarily* or *solely* getting their news from late-night comics. Pew's survey question only asked if the respondent ever learned anything from that type of program, and, if so, how often they learned something. "Do you ever learn anything" is a far cry from "where do you get all your news?"

What is surprising about the Pew survey results however, is how unsurprising they should be to those who pay attention to those comedy TV shows and to news programs in their current incarnations. Originally, talk shows were mostly devoid of political content and, although hosts from Jack Paar to Johnny Carson were not averse to making jokes about politicians, the nature of the content was not overtly politicized. Few researchers prior to the 1990s studied whether audiences claimed they "learned" news from the jokes of late-night comedians. The turning point for talk shows is usually cited as beginning with the 1992 presidential election when Bill Clinton appeared on the *Arsenio Hall Show* while still a candidate. Clinton was the first serious candidate to make a campaign appearance on an entertainment TV show. Since 1992, presidential candidates have frequently made appearances on TV shows that are not traditional forums for political discussion, shows as diverse as *Oprah, Dr. Phil, The Tonight Show with Jay Leno, Late Night with David Letterman* and *Saturday Night Live.* Communications researcher Jeffrey Jones, in *Entertaining Politics,* argues that since the late 1990s there has been a growth of new political entertainment programming that has expanded the boundaries of political discourse beyond a time where politicians would appear occasionally on a popular entertainment program. Jones cites the creations of programs such as *Politically Incorrect with Bill Maher, Dennis Miller Live* and *The Daily Show with Jon Stewart* as creating a new hybrid of political and entertainment programming. Unlike some cultural critics who wish to divide political discourse into serious and frivolous categories (Postman 1986), Jones views this development as an expansion of the political realm but one which allows other voices beyond the so-called experts to engage in political talk in a language that is common to average Americans. "Comedian-hosts with a different license to speak offer political critiques beyond the scope of what news and pundit political talk have previously imagined" (Jones 2005, 14).

Of the three shows Jones examined in his 2005 study, *The Daily Show with Jon Stewart* is a particularly interesting example. While the skit comedy of *Saturday Night Live (SNL)* has come under increasing interest for its effects on the public's perceptions of candidates, the program airs late at night on a weekend and is limited to 40 episodes a year, with only a small portion of the weekly program strictly dedicated to political and/or current event humor.

By contrast, *The Daily Show with Jon Stewart*—which by 2005 has seen six and a half seasons with host Jon Stewart and is in its ninth year of programming overall—produces between 158–161 half-hour, original episodes a year. These shows are broadcast four times a week on the cable network Comedy Central with original episodes showing at 11:00 p.m. Monday through Thursday with multiple rebroadcasts throughout the following day. These rebroadcasts provide viewers who do not stay up late watching TV the ability to watch the original program while it is still timely. While *SNL*, *The Tonight Show*, and *The Late Show* devote only a small portion of their programs to topical humor, nearly all of the content of *The Daily Show* centers around current events, including, as this study will research, the guest interviews.

The format of *The Daily Show* is the result of the merging of several entertainment programming trends, notably the news satire format and the talk show format. Some commentators, and even *The Daily Show's* original creators, have called it a news *parody* rather than a news *satire* program, while cast members have referred to it as both. News parody would be better described as creating false events to highlight the absurdities of real events, which is not a joke tactic often used by *The Daily Show*. However, parsing the difference between parody and satire is notoriously difficult. A literary debate trying to differentiate between the two types of humor has existed for some time. In his footnotes, Jones (2005, 225) dispatches with the distinction this way: "Entering the debates over literary forms of comedic presentation seems unproductive here, as scholars have devoted entire tracts to these debates, often beginning and ending their search in frustration." Heedful of Jones' advice, I will therefore define the humor produced by *The Daily Show* as satire, which is, according to *The American Heritage Dictionary of the English Language, Fourth Edition*, "irony, sarcasm, or caustic wit used to attack or expose folly, vice, or stupidity."

News satire, specifically broadcast news satire, has existed in many different programs as either the basis for an entire program, as in HBO's *Not Necessarily the News*, Canada's *This Hour Has 22 Minutes*, or in small segments on regular comedy programs such as *SNL*'s "Weekend Update"—a part of the show which has been a staple since its inception. The broadcast news satire mimics the conventions of a traditional nightly news broadcast with the image of an "anchor" sitting at the desk reading the news with a graphic over and behind his left shoulder. Of course the anchor is not a reporter or an anchorperson, but a comedian who may be describing real or fake events in a satirical manner so as to invoke the original "true" version in the minds of the audience. Meanwhile the talk show format, which has also been a staple of television programming, contains the usual elements of a couch, a host and an interviewee. Depending on the format of the show, interviews can be serious, silly or even absurdist as in MTV's *The Tom Green Show*. *The Daily Show with Jon Stewart*[1] represents a hybrid of the news satire and the talk show format, with half to two-thirds of the program devoted to news satire and half to one-third devoted to the interview segments with guests.

What is interesting about *The Daily Show* is that it mimics the conventions of a "real" evening news broadcast, both in the opening title credits and the standard anchor-and-desk-with-graphic, so well that perhaps there isn't any real difference between what Stewart does and what "real" anchors do. French Philosopher Jean Baudrillard, in essay "Simulacra and Simulations" (1988), theorizes that we live in a world of simulation, where one cannot tell the difference between the real and simulated. Jon Stewart fakes the news so well that it might as well be real. One question to pose in aping the conventions of the evening news program, is whether some of the respectability in those conventions is transferred to the program? While Jon Stewart repeatedly refers to his program as a "fake news" show he does not actually create false events to highlight the absurdities of real events, but instead uses real events and images in most of his jokes. The satirical newspaper *The Onion* is perhaps a better example of creating false news stories out of whole cloth. The *modus operandi* of *The Daily Show*'s humor is to use real news footage, often obtained from cable news networks, incorporated with the show's writers' interpretive spin on the event. These observations (jokes) may also be sharp and biting, as good political satire should be.

The similarities between *The Daily Show*'s so-called fake news and actual news programs are difficult to ignore. The difference between what is shown on the evening news programs and what is presented on *The Daily Show* often seems only different in tone and style, not of substance. Researcher Diana Mutz of the University of Pennsylvania performed an interesting experiment. Mutz showed one clip of *The Daily Show* to two different groups, telling one they were about to see a clip from a *comedy show* and the other they were about to see a clip from a *news program*. She removed certain cues, such as audience laughter, which would have betrayed the nature of the program. She asked whether the same information, presented in the same form, would have less influence if presented as comedy opposed to news. Her conclusions were that it would not; the impact on the audience was nearly identical (Mutz 2004). This was only a small study however and its conclusions need to be tested further but it is suggestive of the power of the comedy in conveying information, particularly in a format that closely resembles a news program.

Certainly there are cues on both news and comedy programs that the viewer is watching a serious program or a funny one. But the interpretation of the viewer's reaction to the content, in light of those cues, is an excellent topic for research as entertainment, media and news delivery are indelibility intertwined.

What happens when the "news" is presented in an amusing format? *The Daily Show's* unique formatting raises these questions for examination: What exactly is the political content of the program and who is the audience absorbing this content? Who consumes *The Daily Show* and what specifically are they consuming? Are viewers of *The Daily Show* learning from the program or are they seeking amusement and alternative interpretations of news text that a satirist can provide? Sociologist researchers Elihu Katz and Jay Blumler (1974) advanced the theory of uses and gratifications, which furthers the idea that audiences are not just passive viewers of media. Audiences seek out certain texts (be it comedy, drama, news, etc.) for their own purposes. Rather than the media acting upon them, audiences are active participants, taking from texts what they want and discarding viewpoints that are otherwise undesirable. If the program is unbound by conventional news conventions of "fairness" and "balance" to all viewpoints—which is an epistemology in and of itself in the news business—what slant would Stewart bring to his vision of the program?

This project will research all of these questions through various content analyses, public surveys, and statistical analysis. I will examine the political profile of *The Daily Show's* audience as well as the ideological and partisan slant of the program's guest list. I chose to study the guest list of the program because an examination of the guest appearances on entertaining talk shows is one that is long overdue. Most media studies about entertainment talk shows have up until now mainly focused on presidential or candidate appearances. *The Daily Show* has been regularly booking guests from the world of politics well outside of the few appearances by presidential candidates. If the show was attempting to agenda set, as the term is used to apply to the news media (McCombs and Shaw 1972), the guest list would be one method of accomplishing this goal.

H_1: The audience of *The Daily Show* politically leans more towards the Democrats than towards the Republicans.

H_2: The audience of *The Daily Show* is politically more liberal in the aggregate than the aggregated American population.

H_3: The guest list of *The Daily Show* favors Democrats over Republicans.

H_4: The guest list of *The Daily Show* favors guests with left-of-center views over guests with right-of-center views.

H_5: There is a correlation between the political and ideological views of the audience of *The Daily Show* and the majority of the political guests of the program.

Ted Koppel's line to Jon Stewart while on *Nightline* is an example of the nervousness felt by older media personalities towards Stewart's rise in stature, not just as a celebrity, but as a potential rival in the news business. Perhaps it was not shocking when Les Moonves, the co-chief executive of Viacom, which owns both CBS and Comedy Central, publicly speculated in January 2005 about Jon Stewart taking over outgoing *CBS News* anchor Dan Rather's job, even on a part-time basis. Although Moonves eventually backed off from the speculation, the fact that this was even considered within the bounds of normalcy to have a comedian move into Rather's position speaks volumes about the position of authority Stewart might hold. Had Moonves mentioned any other talk show host or comedian, such as David Letterman, who is also a CBS employee, would the reaction have been the same? That David Letterman is not an anchorman might seem obvious to Moonves, but whether Stewart is or is not an anchorman seems a bit unclear. Stewart has said that he is not bound by the conventions of the news room. But he also strenuously denies that his audience is "getting" their news from him, assuming that the jokes on his show require pre-knowledge of events to understand them. While this project will not demonstrate a causal effect between watching *The Daily Show* and increased knowledge of news and politics, it will examine whether there is a correlation between those two variables.

Notes

1 *The Daily Show*'s original host was Craig Kilborn. Entertainment press coverage of the program has noted there were distinct stylistic differences between Jon Stewart's, who took over the program in 1999, and Kilborn's envisioning of the program. This paper will examine some of those differences but from this point all references to *The Daily Show* will refer to the period during which Jon Stewart is host unless otherwise noted.

[...]

6

Issues in Mobile Technology and News Reporting

Sajid Umair

Sajid Umair is a professor of computer science at the National University of Sciences and Technology in Islamabad, Pakistan.

Sajid Umair presents an analysis of the particular benefits and drawbacks of mobile reporting. Made possible by advances in communication technology, mobile reporting has affected newsgathering and reporting in the digital media age, placing greater emphasis on the instantaneous transmittance of news. Umair asserts that it has also allowed for an increase in citizen reporting, making media a more populist field than it has been historically.

The transformation of computing with communication technologies in the past twenty five years has greatly affected the media industry. So the technology for the distribution of journalistic information in various forms has become easily available, offering more opportunities for media societies to reach their audience. Model cross-media publishing describes specifically the steps in the implementation of successful cross-media publication that helps radio and television stations adapt to the ever-changing media market. Cross media is typically defined

"Mobile Reporting and Journalism for Media Trends, News Transmission and Its Authenticity," by Sajid Umair, *Journal of Mass Communication & Journalism*, December 21, 2016. https://www.omicsonline.org/open-access/mobile-reporting-and-journalism-for-media-trends-news-transmissionand-its-authenticity-2165-7912-1000323.pdf. Licensed under CC BY 4.0 International.

by the idea of producing different news including text, videos, and images for more than one media platforms. WWW provides the best transfer of information globally within no time, moreover Wi-Fi and WAP (wireless application protocol) provides users access to online media content and news instantaneously, covering headlines, summaries of recent happenings, and short videos, which provide them the trustworthiness of uploaded content. Content elements make up the publishing network and are categorized into static and dynamic. Static comprises of text, still images and graphics that are then merged for uploading as online content, while dynamic include videos and sounds. The online newscasting is very attractive and allows sources to reach remote viewers quickly. Production of online content via mobile or other devices is an easy task, but its distribution on networks is what makes it challenging. Another important factor is that access to viewers matters the most. The fact that online streaming requires a substantial amount of bandwidth and cost increases with per user accessing it at same time presents a challenge. So high resolution affects the ability to rapidly draw in viewers and make them believe content is coming from a trustworthy source.

Media Publishing

As standard online journalism is trending at an increased rate, readers or viewers appreciate geolocation services that allow them to search for particular news in few seconds. A main criterion in posting online content via mobile is recent and accurate content. During the last few years research in production of journalistic content have been made and termed as mobile journalism, which implies the use of mobile phones in creating and publishing content out of office.

In triple-context-play mobile phones are being used for communication and broadcasting news across world with its audio visual experience and rich multimedia content are considered an optimal application for 3G and mobile internet. The telecommunication industry dominates due to technical usage of mobiles. Using streaming media technology transfer through the mobile communication network, television industry leading mobile multimedia broadcasting technology adoption (CMMB standard, China Mobile Multimedia Broadcasting) through terrestrial and satellite star network transmission for mobile.[18] The innovation and integration in this trend shows the advantages of mobile online content over the old methods.

In the early study of mobile phone communication scholars discussed humanistic trends and compensatory media theory to explain emergence of mobile phones as the phone cut off the people trapped by the landline, satisfying human needs to exchange information and mobile needs, giving our body mobility, plus the ability to connect with the world. Mobiles let us talk to the world and be fully connected. It explored history of mobility in media from reading books to camera phones to transistor radios to laptop, and it and let us converse by voice, image or text.

Mobile Journalism Practice

The first mobile devices equipped with internet access, camera functionality and messaging services became precursors to a growth in using mobile devices for reporting news. More recent technological landmarks have significantly improved such possibilities. This has, on the one hand, led to journalists working for legacy news media adopting such mobile devices in their reporting. On the other, this has also fueled a rapid growth in citizen journalism. Several Nordic studies have explored how mobile technology has created new possibilities for journalism. Some of these have focused on how mobile news reporting influences the organizing and practice of journalism. The peculiar features of mobile devices, such as positioning, have been given specific attention. Additional studies into experimenting with mobile journalism platforms among legacy news media suggest that costs, usability and functionality constitute challenges newsrooms must deal with.[16]

Mobile as a Work Tool

In 2007 the Reuters news agency, seeing the potential of mobile phones, reached an agreement with the company Finnish Nokia, to develop a model for digital journalism. But the big jump came with the emergence of mobile iPhone devices with such advanced features that they became small computers with permanent and specific applications, such as Photoshop.[19] Smartphones are allowing coverage that would have been unthinkable in the past. Up to the present, the only way to send signals was directly linked satellite, terrestrial or microwave. These technologies suffered with difficult terrain, as ground links facilitated telephone communications, transmissions television and other media such as telex, facsimile, etc.[20]

Mobile Journalists

Mobile devices have enhanced the possibilities for journalists to work and report from the field. They can be used for news reporting for mobile news platforms, but also for the entire cross media portfolio. Internet connectivity and advanced search functionality, along with a myriad of intelligent and easily accessible apps, have obviously provided journalists with new and powerful tools for reporting news. Google queries, facts from databases, as well as gateways to informants are typically only a couple of clicks away.[21] For instance, notes empower journalists to instantly double check earlier statements and facts while interviewing a politician. Mobile technology generally stands out as making news reporting more efficient in times when journalists in many legacy news media organizations are shrinking. Mobile journalists are journalists who use mobile devices in their news reporting. Such practices have grown considerably around the globe, from Asia and Australia to Africa, North America and Europe.[22, 23]

Impact of Online and Mobile Technologies on Broadcast Journalism

In order to properly understand the future of television journalism, one must understand how it grew to where it is today. The past tells us that technology causes journalism to change. In the mid nineteenth century, the telegraph allowed news publishers to gather and send information across the globe faster than ever before. By the early twentieth century, the camera could create photographic images of people and events that readers had never been able to see.[24] In the past forty years, most afternoon newspapers have disappeared, people's primary news sources have shifted from paper, to television, to the internet, and our ways of understanding the news has completely changed. Many studies regarding how changing technologies impact broadcast journalism were conducted in the early 2000s, when the internet began to have a strong presence in the world of news media. Since its invention, the internet has become the most popular means of communicating news, and has increasingly changed journalists' job and their impacts on their audience, along with the subsequent advent of mobile technology. In 2001, Bardoel and Deuze further explored the endless technological possibilities of the internet and how a new occupation and industry had been created digital and online journalism. In another study, Deuze analyzed the first generation of news media online to find that online journalism was a fundamentally different type of journalism, particularly because it involved a new platform to share information that must constantly be kept in mind for journalists in the future.[25] As Henry Jenkins correctly predicted in the 2001 MIT technology review, media will be everywhere, and we will use all kinds of media in relation to one another. Giles and Snyder[26] also supported this prediction in problems and prospects of journalism: What's next? By compiling essays from experts in the United States who recognized how journalism would likely change with the internet, and predicted it would be the future of news.[27]

Job Changes Due to Online and Mobile News

Online and mobile technologies play an increasingly prominent role in television newsrooms, particularly on the local level. At this level reporters are responsible for all on-air and web content regarding their story, including a print style web article. On the network level, journalists bring a new value to their website by adding materials beyond the on-air broadcasts. For example, producers at *CBS This Morning* are encouraged to supply web extras to their stories, including parts of stories that did not make it on the air, but may be complementary to the final product online and on mobile platforms, including extra b-roll and parts of interviews.[28] Network producers also deal with complicated copyright issues on the internet. Music, still photographs and footage licensed for particular news or feature segments are often cleared just for television broadcast, but not for the internet. Therefore, some segments are restricted from the web. With that in mind, producers are now trying to secure rights and clearances for both their broadcast and online stories when negotiating for them.[29]

Changes to the Newsroom

As a result of online and mobile news, big changes happened to content production in the newsroom. Matt Howerton, reporter at KWTX in Waco, Texas, called it a balancing act explaining that having to focus on the online and mobile content makes for a much more complicated day for local journalists.[30] But, some stations have taken advantage of the online and mobile audience and created useful content opportunities for the reporter as well as the audience. To adapt to a changing work environment, many newsrooms have added a digital media team, a group of people hired to produce and manage online content, which has become the norm in many local stations and at the network level.[31] Drew Smith, a reporter at WSPA-TV in Spartanburg, South Carolina, believes the digital team is an integral part of the newsgathering and dissemination process of information.[32]

Social Media and Mobile Journalism

Social networks are not just useful tools for journalists, they are also powerful new aggregators and distribution networks, which threaten to further disrupt the already uncertain economics of the internet. The click and link economy has tended to work against traditional publishers, disaggregating content and allowing search engines and web portals to take a significant slice of the available revenues. Now, social networks like Facebook are becoming the portals of the twenty first century: a key starting point for web journeys and a place where audiences are spending more and more time. The popularity and time spent with social networking sites is changing the way people spend their time online and the way in which they share and interact in their daily lives. This is creating new challenges for the media and advertising industries. Social networks provide competition to traditional publishers for consumer attention and at the same time they are opening up new ways of engaging and connecting with audiences. It is important to note that the usage of social sites is highly uneven. A recent Harvard business school survey found that 10 percent of Twitter users generate more than 90 percent of the content and most people have only "tweeted" once.[33] This suggests that many people are using Twitter more as a one way publishing service than a two way, peer to peer communication network. There are three key reasons for the growth of news and information in social networks: 1. Facebook created a news and activity feed in September 2006, which has become a default setting on a user's homepage. This has encouraged more linking to mainstream news sites. It has since made it easier to include links and recommendations from other news related sites. 2. Mainstream audiences are now using social networks and they have brought their interests and preoccupations, including the sharing of news. For this reason experienced Facebook dramatic early growth with global audience (December 2007–December 2008).[34] 3. Websites have provided icons or buttons to allow easy sharing and linking and otherwise promoted social networks. Audio video integration with YouTube has proved a huge boon because of the younger demographic; now news sites are doing the same. Newspapers and media companies have started to establish specialist marketing groups to exploit and monitor the impact of content in these spaces. The *Telegraph* has focused its efforts on targeting specific networks, notably Digg, with which it has a close relationship and very high return click through. The *New York Times* has set up a "Buzz" marketing department, which pays particular attention to the different social networks, and the different audiences they could attract.[1, 35]

Opportunities and Challenges for Journalism

The emergence of the internet together with developments in news aggregation, online search engines and social media has transformed how news is produced, distributed and watched. Newspapers are no longer gatekeepers of access to news. The rise of social media and the ubiquity of online news and opinion constitute an existential challenge to the traditional newspaper model in which professional journalists act as protectors and privileged distributor of information. The pace and scope of the non-organized digital coverage of the most important news of the last decade or so like the Hudson river plane crash in January 2009,[36] the 2004 tsunami, and the attack on the compound of Osama bin Laden in Abbottabad, Pakistan 2011[37] shows the growing power of social media. With the rise of internet online digital/social media publications has changed the picture. The trend in preference is shifting towards briefer news articles and stories shared via mobile based technology. As with citizen journalism, one of the problems with social media is that stories are often not checked. After the floods in China, newspapers used photographs from social media that had been taken a decade earlier. There are many instances of newspapers or news agencies citing social media sources, which are subsequently proven to be incorrect. The future is digital. Subsequently, news organizations will need to cope with tensions between traditional journalism and new approaches, emphasizing speed of output. The primary concern is about exchange and news aggregation in digital world.

Technological advancements in mobiles phones are changing the way journalists report live news and stories. Improved speed and capacity has provided reporters the ability to share online content much quicker and easier than ever before. The potential for news gathering is due to increased mobile phones equipped with cameras, and it made live streaming of videos, photos and other content relatively easy.

MoJo, often known as mobile journalism, makes use of mobile phones for gathering and distributing information containing text, videos, and other content.

Comparison Between TV Reporting and Mobile Journalism

Mobile reporting is usually done by urban citizens with devices like smart phones. It may not be reliable, as someone may perceive information wrong or someone might spread false information intentionally. TV news reporting used to be done using reliable resources. Any news before broadcasting was researched and inquired.

Authenticity of Mobile Reports

As the technology is emerging, the use of mobile phones and cameras for live reporting and journalism have also questioned the authenticity of the content being generated and put on the internet. The use of photo and video sharing sites and blogs and social platform has maximized the inauthenticity of incidents and content. Immediate transmission has increased the competition between professional reporters and amateur eyewitnesses capturing events using their personal devices. The videos and image with low quality and blurred videos are usually considered to be authentic. The videos and photos may be tempered or manipulated or the content may be provided in such a way that it conveys half or wrong information. Videos may be spread by the opposite parties completely providing false information. A major research topic in mobile journalism field is to build methods for checking authenticity and reliability of mobile videos and photos.

Methods Proposed to Authenticate
Information in Mobile Journalism

A common information collecting body can be introduced to collect all the mobile reporting information. Then some criteria should be set for authenticating the content. For example, if more people report about the same information or report, it may be considered reliable.

Furthermore, a new approach to capturing GPS coordinates with pictures can be introduced. Whenever any content is reported, its GPS coordinates can be used to determine location and then authenticity of the content.

Proper laws should be made for mobile journalists. The provider of wrong information or false information should be fined and punished so that the people do not report false content on the internet.

Future Work

New applications can be developed for mobile journalism reporting. Legal bodies can be made to regulate the process. New methods can be introduced to capture videos and photos along with GPS coordinates, which will make the content in mobile journalism and people will refrain from spreading false information via mobile reporting. We can use GPRS to capture images and videos it will help to improve journalism in more effective ways.

Conclusion

Mobile phones have been revolutionizing journalism for quite a long time. First was the emergence of a new actor in the world of information, the citizen journalist, but now reporters are those who have decided to break with the established model and use this tool to inform and give live images from anywhere without the need of broadcast systems through the use of the mobile phone. Emerging professtionals in the field must adapt to this new environment and become polyvalent. The internet and mobile devices have already reformed the newsroom by introducing new means to connect with viewers and to communicate with other journalists within the same place. If embracing this change expands the definition of news from long form broadcast stories to one hundred and forty characters of text, it will create a new lucrative business model. It is clear from this study that social media and user generated content is increasingly moving center stage; influencing the strategic direction and practice of journalism. It is possible to see three distinct phases in the development of community and participation on mainstream websites: (1) The emergence of message boards and community building, (2) Blogging and (3) The rise of social media and social networks. None of these have replaced the previous incarnations, which have continued to evolve in their own right. But in total, we are seeing an unprecedented growth in the amount of participation on mainstream websites, allied to an explosion in self-expression on third party sites. As mobile technology continues to be taken up readily by younger users, ensuring the continued development of the technology as new social uses emerge, it is also an area of particular interest to educators both generally, and particularly in the areas of journalism, media and communications. But this mobile journalism has its limitations: if we come across a huge terrorist attack and all the 3G mobile phone systems are cut off for security reasons, that technology is then a rendered useless. This paper further puts light on how mobile journalism is being used nowadays and to the extent the mobile reporting can be trusted. This paper also discussed issues and limitations of mobile journalism. Mobile journalism is the fastest means of spreading news using social networking sites and video and photo sharing sites. The paper suggested some recommendations for making the content being uploaded on the internet reliable. The restricting and liberating edge of accessibility transforms restaurants, public transport, automobiles, literacy, parent-child relationships, war, and indeed all walks of life, trivial and profound. Like an organic cell that moves, evolves, combines with other cells, and generates, the mobile phone has become a complex sparkplug of human life.

References

1. Nicole C (2014) Revolutionizing the Newsroom: How Online and Mobile Technologies Have Changed Broadcast Journalism. *The Elon Journal of Undergraduate Research in Communications* 5: 1-3.

2. http://www.efc.be/event/coop-break-light-my-fire-the-energy-transition-anopportunity-for-cooperative-energy-production/

3. Wright CR (1960) Functional Analysis and Mass Communication. *Public Opinion Quarterly* 24: 605-620.

4. Cameron D (2011) Mobile journalism: A snapshot of current research and practice. In: Charles A, Stewart G (eds.) *The end of journalism: News in the twenty-first century.* Peter Lang Publisher, Switzerland pp: 63-71.

5. Castells M, Fernandez-AM, Qiu J, Sey A (2004) The mobile communication society: a cross cultural analysis of available evidence on the social use of wireless communication technology. Annenberg Research Network on International Communication, Los Angeles, USA.

6. http://www.pewresearch.org

7. http://www.pewinternet.org/fact-sheets/mobile-technology-fact-sheet

8. Westlund O (2008) From Mobile Phone to Mobile Device. News Consumption on the Go. *Canadian Journal of Communication* 33: 443-463.

9. http://www.tandfonline.com/doi/full/10.1080/21670811.2012.740273

10. Wei R, Louis L (1999) Blurring public and private behaviors in public space: policy challenges in the use and improper use of the cell phone. *Telematics and Informatics* 16: 11-26.

11. Wei R (2008) Motivations for Using the Mobile Phone for Mass Communications and Entertainment. *Telematics and Informatics* 25: 36-46.

12. Leung LRW (1999) Seeking News via the Pager: An Expectancy Value Study. *Journal of Broadcasting and Electronic Media* 43: 299-315.

13. Ful JH, Chang JH, Huang YM, Chao HC(2012) A Support Vector Regressionbased Prediction of Students' School Performance. 2012 International Symposium on Computer, Consumer and Control 84-87.

14. http://www.reuters.com/

15. http://theendofjournalism.wdfiles.com/local--files/davidcameron/David%20Cameron.pdf

16. Jokela T, Heliva J, Tiina K (2009) Mobile Journalist Toolkit: A Field Study on Producing News Articles with a Mobile Device. Proceedings of MindTrek'09.

17. Mills J, Paul E, Omer R, Heli V (2012) MoJo in Action: The Use of Mobiles in Conflict, Community, and Crossplatform Journalism.. Continuum. 26: 669-683.

18. Interfax (2006) China releases mobile TV industrial standard in Interfax China.

19. http://www.computerworld.com/article/3056191/apple-ios/hands-on-for-theipad-pro-smaller-is-big.html

20. http://press.princeton.edu/chapters/i8885.html

21. Bivens RK (2008) The Internet, Mobile Phones and Blogging. Journalism Practice 2: 113-129.

22. Stephen Q (2009) MoJo: Mobile in the Asian Region. KonradAdenauerStiftung, Singapore 1-65.

23. Mabweazara HM (2009) Between the Newsroom and the Pub: The Mobile Phone in the Dynamics of Everyday Mainstream Journalism Practice 2009. *Journalism* 12: 692-707.

24. http://www.studentpulse.com/articles/969/revolutionizing-the-newsroom-howonline-and-mobile-technologies-have-changed-broadcast-journalism

25. Dooley PL (2007) *The Technology of Journalism: Cultural Agents, Cultural Icons.* Northwestern University Press,USA.

26. Bardoel J, Deuze Mark (2001) Network Journalism: Converging Competences of Media Professionals and Professionalism. *Australian Journalism Review* 23: 91-103.

27. Giles R, Snyder, Robert W (2001) *Problems & Prospects of Journalism: What's Next?* Transaction Publishers, USA.

28. http://www.journalism.org/2013/10/11/how-americans-get-tv-news-at-home/

29. http://www.koat.com/tv/news-team/General-Assignment-Reporter/27107354

30. https://www.theguardian.com/media-network/media-network-blog/2014/ sep/29/technology-changing-marketing-digital-media

31. Deborah PKEM, Amy M (2013) Local TV: Audience Declines as Revenue Bounces Back. The State of the News Media 2013.

32. http://www.hbs.edu

33. http://www.mediatrust.org/about-us/news/news-archive-2007/

34. Zhang L (2009) Does state funding affect graduation rates at public four year colleges and universities? *Educational Policy* 23: 714-731.

35. Marra PPCJD, Dolbeer R, Dahlan NF (2009) Migratory Canada geese cause crash of US Airways Flight 1549. Front Ecol Environ 7:97-301.

36. http://onlinelibrary.wiley.com/doi/10.1029/2005EO040002/full

37. Miller G (2011) CIA spied on bin Laden from safe house, in the *Washington Post.*

7

Quality and Profitability in the News Business

Marc Gunther

Marc Gunther is a writer at Fortune Magazine *who focuses on network television and issues in journalism. He is the author of* The House That Roone Built: The Inside Story of ABC News.

In this viewpoint, Marc Gunther examines the changes in media content that have occurred over the past three decades as corporate influence has increased in the news industry. In particular, he examines the tension between quality-based and profitability-based metrics as they have been applied to journalism and other media content. Gunther asserts that network news has remained influential in spite of changes in the news industry, but that adaptation is necessary for survival. He argues that although the focus so far has been on profitability, a greater emphasis on quality will ultimately be necessary.

Twenty years ago, there was no network news "business." The Big Three broadcast television networks—ABC, CBS and NBC—all covered news, but none generally made money doing so. Nor did they expect to turn a profit from news programming. They presented news programming for the prestige it would bring to their network, to satisfy the public-service requirements of Congress and the Federal Communications Commission, and more broadly so that they would be seen as good corporate citizens.

"The Transformation of Network News," by Marc Gunther, President and Fellows of Harvard College. Published by arrangement with the Nieman Foundation for Journalism.

Back then, the networks earned enough money from entertainment programming that they could afford to run their news operations at a loss. And so they did. Former CBS correspondent Marvin Kalb recalls Owner and Chairman William Paley instructing news reporters at a meeting in the early 1960's that they shouldn't be concerned about costs. "I have Jack Benny to make money," he told them.

It is no exaggeration to say that just about everything has changed since then. Today, ABC, CBS and NBC operate in a competitive environment in which most viewers have dozens of channels from which to choose. That has transformed not just TV news but the entire television industry. Those most severely threatened by the way the broadcast business operates are the Big Three. The ABC and CBS networks (now subsumed into larger corporate structures) are losing money, according to Wall Street analysts. NBC's network profits are also falling sharply. Those who own these networks—Disney (ABC), CBS Inc. with its major stockholder, Mel Karmazin, and General Electric (NBC)—all demand that their news operations make money.

This demand for profit arises not because these owners are greedier than their predecessors were, but because the financial challenges they face are tougher. The TV entertainment business, in particular, has deteriorated because programming costs are rising while, due to more competition, ratings are falling and hit shows are harder to find. All of this leaves the TV entertainment business struggling to find its way. The networks' entertainment and sports operations are so troubled that news, particularly in prime time, is becoming one of the networks' most consistently profitable businesses. To some extent, news programs are now looked to as ways to subsidize entertainment and sports offerings— just the reverse of the way things used to be.

What do such changes mean for the practice of journalism at the Big Three? Is this possibly the best of times for network news, since as the news becomes more profitable, its status will rise within the corporation, and with increased status will come a finer product? Or is this a troubled time for network news, as old-fashioned values of public service that once guided news judgment cede ground to business-driven imperatives? Most importantly, given the current economic climate, how best can journalists respond to these corporate, societal and technological changes and preserve the quality and integrity of news?

Network News Still Matters

Because so much has been written recently about the decline of the Big Three and the rise of cable and the Internet, it is worth observing that network news still matters. In turn, what stories the Big Three choose to broadcast and how they tell them also still matters.

During 1998, the three evening newscasts reached a combined average of about 30.4 million viewers in 22 million homes. This represents a reach that is greater than the total circulation of the nation's 10 largest newspapers. Prime-time news programs connect with even larger audiences. CBS's *60 Minutes* (Sunday), the industry leader, has attracted an average of 13.4 million homes so far during the 1998-99 TV season. And *60 Minutes* is only one of 14 prime-time, hour-long news shows appearing on the Big Three. No cable program or newspaper has anything approaching that kind of reach. The most popular cable news program, CNN's *Larry King Live*, is seen by fewer than one million homes on a typical night. The Big Three networks are still, by far, the most commanding voices in American journalism and therefore one of the most important forces in our democracy.

Finding the Formula for Profits

The evolution of network news into a profit-making business unfolded gradually, driven by a series of events dating back more than two decades. The success of *60 Minutes*, which became a Nielsen top 10 program in the 1977-78 season, 10 years after its debut, was an enormously influential factor. To compete against entertainment shows in prime time, Don Hewitt, the show's creator, knew that he had to produce something that wasn't a traditional news program. It would not be built around the important news of the day (or the week), but would be a weekly series that emphasized storytelling, introduced journalists as protagonists, and created drama around their exposing bad guys or tangling with the powerful and famous. "There are TV shows about doctors, cowboys, cops," Hewitt once said. "This is a show about four journalists. But instead of actors playing these four guys, they are themselves." With this formula, *60 Minutes* became the first successful prime-time newsmagazine. As such, it was also the first news program to generate big profits for a network. Given this combination, it became a harbinger of things to come.

[...]

[Networks] focused sustained attention for the first time in the news divisions on controlling spending. They hired management consultants to analyze costs and look for cuts. Andrew Heyward, now President of CBS News, says: "There had been a long period during which the news budgets were very generous, and there was not a lot of attention paid. There's no question that in the latter half of the 1980's, certainly at this place, there was a new emphasis on the cost of producing the news."

The formula for making network news into a profitable business was thus established:

- Make the product more entertaining. As Hewitt proved with *60 Minutes*, when you tell stories in ways that engage the audience, often by touching their emotions, news programming can generate high ratings and revenues.
- Produce more programming. As Arledge established, in business terms a network news operation can be seen as a factory with a lot of fixed costs: bureaus, studios, equipment, correspondents, producers, editors, executives and network overhead. The more programs that the factory can churn out, the more revenues can be generated to recoup these set costs. Once those fixed costs have been paid for, the marginal costs of producing more hours become relatively low.

- Control spending. Wright, Tisch and Capital Cities did this, and today's owners are continuing to do it. The networks have, among other things, closed foreign and domestic bureaus, laid off staff, eliminated some money-losing documentary units, and curbed convention and election coverage.

[...]

Cutting Costs

With their newscasts' ratings slipping and revenues flat, news divisions, looking to increase profits, feel they have had little choice but to control the costs of gathering news. Layoffs have become periodic occurrences during the past decade. During the fall of 1998, all the networks reduced staff. CBS was hardest hit, eliminating about 120 positions from its 1,600-person news staff; most were technical, office and managerial people, not correspondents and producers. ABC thinned its executive ranks, and some high-paid correspondents and producers were also let go. NBC imposed a hiring freeze in news, as well as in the rest of the company, after the network lost its biggest moneymaker, *Seinfeld*, and negotiated a contract with its leading prime-time drama, *ER*, that required huge per-episode fees.

"If I told you that there was a date certain when we were going to stop cutting costs, you shouldn't believe me," says David Westin, the President of ABC News. "It's an ongoing process." Ongoing, indeed. Several experienced, hard-news correspondents, people such as medical specialist George Strait, legal correspondent Tim O'Brien, and former Hong Kong Bureau Chief Jim Laurie have left or are about to leave ABC News.

One problem the networks face as they cut back is that breaking news is unpredictable. Like firehouses, news bureaus need to be staffed for emergencies, but often the correspondents and producers are idle. Stationing people in distant locales is inherently inefficient. Even when big stories erupt, some inefficiency is inevitable. As CBS's Heyward explains: "If you're going to gather news around the world, that's not inherently profitable the way creating a newsmagazine is. When you create a newsmagazine, most everything you produce gets on the screen—you can choose what to cover, and that's very efficient. But if you're running a London bureau, even if you run it lean and mean, when there's a threat of war in Iraq, you're going there. You put somebody on the cruiser or on the battleship without knowing how many pieces he or she is going to generate."

Each network defines what it calls a "bureau" differently, and staffers are shifted with some regularity. This makes it hard to obtain comparable data on how many bureaus have been closed and how many remain. In October 1998, ABC News had five foreign bureaus staffed with correspondents. CBS News had four. And NBC News had seven, according to the *New York Times*. By comparison, CNN had 23. What is clear is that the Big Three have retrenched. None still has a full-time correspondent stationed in southeast Asia, Central or South America, or sub-Saharan Africa, except for staffers shared by CBS's Spanish-language arm, CBS Telenoticias. Domestic bureaus have also been closed. Rather than maintain full-time staff in far-flung outposts, the networks have found ways to obtain what they call "generic" coverage— images that are widely available—from outside sources. They use footage from foreign networks, from their own affiliates, even from independent suppliers such as NewsTV, a company that provides coverage to the networks from its headquarters in Lawrence, Kansas.

"We're building an empire on being the Kelly Girls of network news," says Russ Ptacek, a former local TV reporter who is President of NewsTV. Even programs that don't rely totally on hard news, such as *20/20* and *Today*, use his 26-person operation, he says, because "the only time the networks are paying for our services is when we're on location, working for them."

Last year, ABC, NBC and CBS each had discussions with CNN about sharing staff and bureaus outside of the United States. While a full-fledged merger between a broadcast network and CNN, now part of Time Warner, appears unlikely, increased cooperation of some kind seems inevitable. The technique of "pooling," in which news operations share footage from a single camera as they do in Congress and at the White House, has already begun to spread overseas. "Internationally, you will probably see some consolidation of resources," says Pat Fili-Krushel, the President of ABC, who oversees ABC News.

The networks argue that they don't need as many bureaus and reporters now because their role has changed. Rather than trying to be first on the air with a headline or a picture, the mission at ABC, CBS and NBC is defined as providing so-called value-added programming—in-depth analysis and original reporting that 24-hour cable services and local TV can't duplicate. This makes sense, but it's difficult to provide thoughtful reporting of stories around the nation and the world without reporters on the ground who are given the resources to develop expertise. Paul Friedman, Executive Producer of ABC's *World News Tonight*, says, "Journalism is about going out and looking at things, and you can't do that by buying video from APTV…. You wind up doing a lot more of what we did before the news budgets expanded and that was parachute in. If you have good people who have a lot of experience, you can generally parachute in and do a good job. But it is not the same as having somebody on the ground who calls you and says, you know, you really ought to come and look at this developing story." The same goes for coverage in Washington, where specialized beats have been gradually eliminated or several assignments have been combined.

The war in Yugoslavia in the spring of 1999 exemplifies some of the problems that accompany these new approaches to network news coverage. No network had been covering the emerging crisis in Kosovo on an ongoing basis. Few reporters knew Serbian President Slobodan Milosevic, knew much about the tensions fueling the crisis, or had established sources in the region. Even the best correspondents covering the NATO bombing and the mass eviction of Albanians were new to this story. When the Pentagon and the Serbs both clamped down on information, many in the press were largely unprepared to cover aspects of this story and, as a consequence, many critics felt the public was ill served.

[...]

The Quality Solution

On one theme, the three network news presidents agree. No matter how the television landscape changes, they insist, viewers will continue to be attracted to high-quality news programming. This may sound like wishful thinking, but it is borne out by history. Programs like CBS's *60 Minutes* and ABC's *Nightline*, which are admired for their consistent quality, are also among the most profitable and long-lasting franchises in television. The same is true for NBC's *Today*, which earns about $50 million a year in profits for the network. Its first half-hour is filled with hard news, including overseas and Washington coverage, that is well-produced and timely.

"Good journalism is good business," says NBC's Lack. "*60 Minutes, Nightline* and the *Today* show are these unique programs that go back for...years, that are just embedded in the national consciousness as very reliable, quality programs. Each of us is fortunate to have one of those franchises. They're pillars." In fact, unlike dramas and sitcoms, which run out of steam and leave the air, established news programs seem able to go on for decades. CBS's Heyward says news programs offer "a wonderful combination of the familiar and the new," familiar faces and formats, renewed daily or weekly with new headlines and fresh stories. Says Westin: "They go on forever, you don't have to reinvent them, and they draw an audience, week after week, month after month." In an industry in which four out of five new entertainment programs fail, a successful news program becomes a jewel worth protecting.

The trouble is that creating a franchise like *Today* or *60 Minutes* or *Nightline* is no easy feat, especially now. Network presidents say they want quality, but will they be able to deliver? Consider some obstacles they face:

- The pool of talent is thin. Anchors such as Mike Wallace and Ted Koppel don't come along every day. Nor do executive producers like Don Hewitt and Tom Bettag. It's interesting to note that today's network "stars"—Wallace, Koppel, Rather, Jennings and Brokaw, or Hewitt and Bettag behind the scenes—came of age during the era when TV news was hard-news oriented and shaped by the old values of public service. Each served long apprenticeships covering breaking news: Jennings and Koppel spent years overseas, Rather and Brokaw covered Washington when government and politics were more important to the networks, and Hewitt and Bettag polished their craft producing CBS's flagship evening newscast. Such training is now largely a thing of the past. Many young producers and correspondents are rushed into prime time where the values are market-driven. It is telling that when ABC decided it had to try and save *Good Morning America* it turned to familiar faces, Charles Gibson and Diane Sawyer, who were trained in the old school.

• New programs need time to develop. From network executives, new programs require patience, a faith in the eventual audience and, often, a willingness to experiment. *60 Minutes* took nearly a decade to ripen into a hit show; the show was tolerated for years because CBS was so profitable that it didn't need to maximize revenues during every hour of the broadcast day. *Nightline* arose out of the Iranian hostage crisis, when ABC was willing to commit to late night coverage in order to grab attention and enhance its news image; such a scenario would be highly unlikely today, with networks having all but ceded extensive special-events coverage to the all-news cable networks.

• Quality programs depend on a special bond between the networks and their viewers. In essence, viewers need to believe that the networks are the place to turn for intelligent, thoughtful television journalism. This is the notion behind "branding," which is so valued in business today and has been an important part of the tradition of network news. For all their flaws, the network news divisions for years differentiated themselves from local TV news or syndicated programs because they promised and delivered a product that was perceived as having integrity and quality. The success of magazines such as *20/20* and *Dateline* stems partly from the power of their network brands; viewers who trust NBC News or ABC News, after years of watching Brokaw, Jennings and Koppel, believe that they can expect the same quality in prime time. The danger, of course, is that the primetime feature and infotainment programs will fail to meet those expectations, and the value of the network brands could erode.

The question now is, given all the changes and pressures occurring in the news broadcast industry, whether a culture of journalism still exists at the networks to surmount these obstacles and achieve real "brand" quality. Can a new generation of stars with journalistic experience, authority and skill emerge from the plethora of feature prime-time magazine programming to match the quality of the now-aging cohort of network stars? Do the networks still have the patience to support a high quality news program such as *Nightline* or *60 Minutes* through years—not to mention a decade—of losing money until it builds a loyal audience base? And, more importantly, will any of the networks invest what it takes to fulfill their commitment to comprehensively informing the public about the major issues and events of our time once they have established new bonds with viewers?

The networks probably have a greater stake now in developing the highest quality talent, in demonstrating patience, and in protecting their brands if they want to maintain a loyal cadre of viewers from among the splintering audience. With the proliferation of channel choices, no news division can afford to settle for second-rate programming. The best programs and brands will survive and even thrive in this cluttered environment. It's a good bet that viewers will continue to seek out *60 Minutes*, but it's not clear whether they'll hunt for *Dateline* or *20/20*, which are more dependent on hype, gimmicks and stories that pander to their audiences. If news becomes available on demand and for a fee (as it might), some people will probably pay to watch *Nightline*, as long as it retains its excellence.

The economic forces now buffeting the business of network news are unlikely to abate. Viewers and advertisers will continue to have more, not fewer, choices in where to turn for their news and marketing. Profit pressures at network news divisions will intensify, not diminish. In this unforgiving environment, the question is whether the core requirements necessary to provide solid journalism—time to pursue stories and develop sources, a recognition that not all coverage is going to produce immediate profit, an ability to focus on important topics that won't bring high ratings but can build viewer trust—can be sustained. If history holds true that audiences in the long run gravitate to quality, network aspirations will not be enough. The networks will need to take the risk and time to invest in quality.

8

Drawbacks of the Digital News Media Environment

Dan Kennedy

Dan Kennedy is an associate professor of journalism at Northeastern University and a participant in the WGBH "Beat the Press" panel.

Dan Kennedy argues that the decline of the traditional newspaper business model has resulted in a major decline in access to quality journalism. He is pessimistic that online business models will ever be viable for newspapers, predicting that they will continue to be forced to cut costs and operate on as little money as possible. Fundamental changes need to be made in order to allow the newspaper industry to stay afloat, as charging to read online content will not accomplish this.

Twenty years ago this month, the *New York Times* entered the Internet age with a sense of optimism so naive that looking back might break your heart. "With its entry on the Web," wrote *Times* reporter Peter H. Lewis, "The *Times* is hoping to become a primary information provider in the computer age and to cut costs for newsprint, delivery and labor."

The *Times* wasn't the first major daily newspaper to launch a website. The *Boston Globe*, then owned by the New York Times Co., had unveiled its Boston.com service—featuring free content from the *Globe* and other local news organizations—just a few

"Print Is Dying, Digital Is No Savior: The Long, Ugly Decline of the Newspaper Business Continues Apace," by Dan Kennedy, WGBH News, January 26, 2016. Reprinted by permission.

months earlier. But the debut of NYTimes.com sent a clear signal that newspapers were ready to enlist in the digital revolution.

Fast-forward to 2016, and the newspaper business is a shell of its former self. Far from cutting newsprint and delivery costs, newspapers remain utterly reliant on their shrunken print editions for most of their revenues—as we have all been reminded by the *Globe*'s home-delivery fiasco.

Not only do newspapers remain tethered to 20th-century industrial processes such as massive printing presses, tons of paper, and fleets of delivery trucks, but efforts to develop new sources of digital revenue have largely come to naught.

Craigslist came up with a new model for classified ads—free—with which newspapers could not compete. And there went 40 percent of the ad revenue.

Digital display advertising has become so ubiquitous that its value keeps dropping. Print advertising still pays the bills, but for how much longer? The Internet has shifted the balance of power from publishers to advertisers, who can reach their customers far more efficiently than they could by taking a shot in the dark on expensive print ads. The result, according to the Newspaper Association of America (as reported by the Pew Research Center), is that print ad revenues have fallen from $44.9 billion in 2003 to just $16.4 billion in 2014, while digital ad revenues—$3.5 billion in 2014—have barely budged since 2006.

And it's getting worse. Last week Richard Tofel, president of the nonprofit news organization ProPublica and a former top executive with the *Wall Street Journal*, wrote an essay for *Medium* under the harrowing headline "The sky is falling on print newspapers faster than you think." Tofel took a look at the 25 largest US newspapers and found that their print circulation is continuing to drop at a rapid rate, contrary to predictions that the decline had begun to level off.

There's a bit of apples-and-oranges confusion in Tofel's numbers. For instance, he suggests that the 140,000 paid weekday print circulation that the *Globe* claimed in September 2015 was somehow analogous to the 115,000 it reported during the recent home-delivery crisis. In fact, according to the Alliance for Audited Media, the *Globe* had 119,000 home-delivery and mail customers in September 2015. (Another 30,000 or so print newspapers were sold via single-copy sales.)

But there's no disputing Tofel's bottom line, which is that print circulation plunged between 2013 and 2015 at a far faster rate than had been expected. The *Journal* is down by 400,000; the *Times* by 200,000; the *Washington Post* and the *Los Angeles Times* by 100,000.

"Nearly everyone in publishing with whom I shared the 2015 paid figures found them surprisingly low," Tofel wrote, adding that "if print circulation is much lower than generally believed, what basis is there for confidence the declines are ending and a plateau lies ahead?"

If advertising is falling off the cliff and print circulation is plummeting, then surely the solution must be to charge readers for digital subscriptions, right? Well, that may be part of the solution. But it's probably not realistic to think that such a revenue stream will ever amount to much more than a small part of what's needed to run a major metropolitan newspaper.

Not everyone agrees, of course. The journalist and entrepreneur Steven Brill, in a recent interview with Poynter.org, said newspaper executives find themselves in their current straits because they were not nearly as aggressive as they should have been about building paywalls around their content.

"I always had a basic view ... that if you weren't getting revenue from readers, you ultimately weren't going to put a premium on your journalism," said Brill, a founder of the paywall company Press Plus, which he later sold. "You couldn't just rely on advertisers because they would then be your only real customers."

Brill's views are not extreme. For instance, he thinks it's reasonable to give away five to 10 articles a month, as newspapers with metered paywalls such as the *Globe* and the *Times* do. But Brill does not mention what I think are by far the two biggest hurdles newspapers face in charging for digital content.

First, customers are already paying hundreds of dollars a month for broadband, cell service, and their various digital devices. It's not crazy for them to think that the content should come included with that, as it does (for the most part) with their monthly cable bill. Those who wag their fingers that newspapers never should have given away their content overlook the reality that customers had none of those extra expenses back when their only option was to pay for the print edition.

Second, paywalls interfere with the way we now consume news—skipping around the Internet, checking in with multiple sources. To wall off content runs contrary not just to what news consumers want but to the sharing culture of the Internet. The *Globe* has had quite a bit of success is selling digital subscriptions— about 90,000, according to the September 2015 audit report. But what will happen when the paper ratchets the price up to $1 a day, as the newspaper analyst Ken Doctor recently reported for the website *Newsonomics*?

As I write this, I am on my way to Philadelphia, where I'll be learning more about the transfer of that city's newspapers—the *Philadelphia Inquirer* and the tabloid *Daily News*—to a nonprofit foundation. Ken Doctor, writing for the *Nieman Journalism Lab*, isn't optimistic: "Sprinkling some nonprofit pixie dust won't save the newspaper industry. Only new ideas can do that."

For the beleaguered newspaper business, the walls are closing in and the oxygen is being pumped out of the room. Clay Shirky, who writes about digital culture, once said, "Society doesn't need newspapers. What we need is journalism."

Trouble is, 20 years after NYTimes.com staked out its home on the web, newspapers are still the source of most of the public interest journalism we need to govern ourselves in a democracy.

9

Benefits of a Diverse and Creative Media Environment

Sarah J. Burton

Sarah J. Burton holds a master's degree in media studies from the Pennsylvania State University Graduate School College of Communications.

In this viewpoint, Sarah J. Burton argues that diversity within the media landscape (including satire and news/comedy) can promote greater deliberation, along with other democratic values. She looks at how new media trends reflect central topics in democratic theory going back to the Greek philosophers. Burton asserts that a mediaocracy— in which media corporations tell the public what to think about issues—is harmful to the public, and satirical news sources help to take some of this power away from media corporations.

If entertainment media are becoming a more popular form of news dissemination, media malaise of such television is in direct conflict with deliberative democracy. This malaise connotes that the viewers simply swallow the news that is being fed to them without any discursive reaction. As Neil Postman feared, the citizenry is being numbed by entertainment. However, as we shall see, this is not the case with every form of entertainment media. Satirical news can elicit meaningful debate. This view—that satire

"'More Than Entertainment': The Role of Satirical News in Dissent, Deliberation, and Democracy," by Sarah J. Burton, December 2010. Reprinted by permission.

is beneficial to the public because it encourages debate—assumes that deliberative democracy is an ideal state of citizenry.

Deliberative Democracy

Deliberative democracy is the focus of a multitude of recent literature. Scholar John Elster noted, "The idea of deliberative democracy, or decision making by discussion among free and equal citizens, is having a revival."[1] Its roots are as deep as the roots of democracy itself. Pericles declared in fifth century B.C.E. that in Athens, discussion is "an indispensable preliminary to any wise action at all."[2] The concept was also revived in the early years of the United States' existence. In the nineteenth-century John Stuart Mill envisioned a government by public discourse, noting that people were no longer barbarians: "Mankind have become capable of being improved by free and equal discussion."[3] Discussion can help the public substitute truth for error, or at the very least, leave a "clearer perception and livelier impression of truth."[4]

More recently, researchers have attempted to define the process of deliberation more specifically. Susan Stokes' definition has particular salience when it comes to the topic of media: Deliberation is "the endogenous change of preferences resulting from communication."[5] Such deliberation occurs through the search for truth, a role that the news media is theoretically supposed to support.[6] However, this definition allows a wide range of communication to fit under deliberation umbrella; it is also the most applicable toward the study of satirical news and its ability to encourage public debate.

Professor Frank Michelman described the actions citizens take when engaging in deliberative democracy: "Participants direct their arguments toward arriving at a reasonable answer to some question of public ordering . . . ."[7] Objectivity need not be discoverable in such a democracy, instead the aim is toward "conciliation within reason" and not "dissolution of difference."[8] Adam Przeworski illustrated the tendency for elite groups, such as politicians and the media, to impose beliefs in the guise of deliberation that benefit only themselves, not the general public.[9] True deliberative democracy, in summation, is viewed as an ideal form of democracy. It is a form that bridges the gaps between the elite and the common man by allowing the common man to question and discuss the beliefs being "imposed" from above. Media should serve the purpose of encouraging deliberative democracy.

James Fearon,[10] Joshua Cohen,[11] and James Johnson[12] all asserted that while improving the intellect of the participating citizen cannot be the reason for choosing the deliberative decision-making procedure, it might be a by-product. In terms of satirical news, the entertainment value may serve as a reason for choosing this format to learn about politics; through questioning and attacking elitist beliefs, the desirable by-product of watching such shows is to become more deliberative in decision-making.

Mediaocracy

Nonetheless, most scholarship views the growth of entertainment in news and the unprecedented power of the media in a negative light. Journalist Danny Schechter defined the rise of "mediaocracy" as the expansion of the "rule by the agenda setting power of privately owned media corporations."[13] In effect, the mediaocracy utilizes propaganda, feeding viewers an opinion repeated in the news echo chamber without any meaningful discourse. Mediaocracy is also disparagingly referred to as "infotainment,"[14] which generally refers to media content mixed with entertainment to enhance popularity.[15] Studies have shown that although more people are turning to infotainment, such as Oprah and other talk shows, for their political news, there is not a positive association between infotainment and the intent to vote or the desire for interpersonal political discussion.[16] Matthew Baum noted that soft news and infotainment are not associated with enhanced long-term store of political knowledge.[17]

Most of the scholarly concerns with infotainment deal with its encroachment into the field of news. Neil Postman, as discussed in the introduction, feared that infotainment was preferencing televisual spectacles over critical information.[18] Of course he was not alone; both David Altheide[19] and Doris Graber[20] argued that news was being packaged into emotion-invoking dramas since they made for a more marketable story line. Part of infotainment and the mediaocracy's emergence is enabled by a changing media landscape of simultaneous fragmentation and integration. Fragmentation occurs because of the evolving technologies and growing number of channels whereby the public can access its news. Integration is happening on an economic level with ownership of media now in "the hands of a small number of giant corporate conglomerates."[21] These corporate conglomerates seek to streamline the media process by regurgitating certain media frames, thereby generating revenue and cutting costs. Robert McChesney and John Nichols concluded that the present-day mediaocracy is the summation of years of commercial media ownership: "[T]he commercial system of journalism that has defined and dominated our discourse for the past 150 years has entered the rapid process of decline that will not be reversed."[22]

However, not all messages in infotainment dumb down the citizenry, and not all news in the mediaocracy must be classified as propaganda. In his book *Entertaining the Citizenry*, Liesbet Van Zoonen wrote, "[T]here are good and bad expressions of politics in popular culture. The good ones may achieve a political awareness that other means of communication rarely produce."[23] Although Zoonen does not specifically identify these types of good expression in popular culture, satirical news programs fit neatly into her description. The importance of pleasure, entertainment, and fun are all regularly ignored when discussing deliberative democracy;[24] hence, the significance of these satirical news shows in relation to deliberative democracy has been similarly overlooked. Popular culture, Zoonen alleged, can encourage deliberation by virtue of it being popular. Shows like *The Daily Show* and *The Colbert Report*, which bring in audiences of over two million,[25] clearly fit this mold.

The revival of theories on deliberative democracy also has implications for First Amendment theory. The concept of free speech must be reevaluated as to encourage the spread of opinions and facts. Since *Hustler Magazine v. Falwell*[26] (1988), when Chief Justice William Rehnquist declared that the speech important for the "public discourse" can be outrageous or profoundly invasive of its target, the Supreme Court has continued to evaluate free speech in such a way to encourage diverse opinion and deliberation.[27] This First Amendment jurisprudence has been defined as individualistic by scholar Robert C. Post: "Individuals must be free within public discourse from the enforcement of all civility rules, so as to be able to advocate and to exemplify the creation of new forms of communal life in their speech."[28] Since the definition of civility changes with the decades, often seemingly outrageous speech is simply ahead of the times. This forward-looking stance is often seen in many types of comedy, including satire. Deliberative democracy looks beyond the aggregation of static majority preferences to the gradual evolution of preferences by way of public discourse.[29] Comedic, outrageous, humorous, and satirical expression thus can be said to be leading the evolution of public discourse.

[…]

Notes

1. John Elster, introduction to *Deliberative Democracy*, (Cambridge: Cambridge University Press, 1998), 1.

2. Thucydides, *The History of the Peloponnesian War: The Second Book*, trans. Richard Crawley, 431 B.C.E., accessed February 14, 2010, http://classics.mit.edu/Thucydides/pelopwar.2.second.html.

3. John Stuart Mill, *On Liberty*, (London: Longman, Roberts & Green, 1869) accessed February 10, 2010, www.bartleby.com/130/.

4. Ibid.

5. Susan Stokes, "Pathologies of Deliberation," in *Deliberative Democracy*, ed. John Elster, (Cambridge: Cambridge University Press, 1998), 123–139.

6. Jack Fuller, *News Values: Ideas for an Information Age*, (Chicago: University of Chicago Press, 1996). See chapter one, "The Truth of the News."

7. Frank Michelman, "Conception of Democracy in America Constitutional Argument: Voting Rights," *Florida Law Review* 41 (1989): 447.

8. Ibid., 448.

9. Adam Przeworksi, "Deliberation and Ideological Domination," in *Deliberative Democracy*, ed. John Elster, (Cambridge: Cambridge University Press, 1998), 140–160.

10. James Fearon, "Deliberation as Discussion," in *Deliberative Democracy*, ed. John Elster, (Cambridge: Cambridge University Press, 1998), 45.

11. Joshua Cohen, "Democracy and Liberty," in *Deliberative Democracy*, ed. John Elster, (Cambridge: Cambridge University Press, 1998), 186.

12. James Johnson, "Arguing for Deliberation: Some Skeptical Considerations," in *Deliberative Democracy*, ed. John Elster, (Cambridge: Cambridge University Press, 1998), 172.

13. Danny Schechter, *The Death of Media: And the Fight to Save Democracy*, (Hoboken: Melville House, 2005).

14. "Primarily a pejorative term, infotainment is often used to denote the decline of hard news and public affairs discussion programs and the corresponding development of a variety of entertainment shows that mimic the style of news." See Geoffrey Baym, "Infotainment," in *The International Encyclopedia of Communication*, ed. Wolfgang Donsbach, Blackwell Reference Online, accessed November 1, 2010, http://www .communicationencyclopedia.com/subscriber/tocnode?id=g9781405131995_chunk_g9 78140513199514_ss32-1.

15. David Demers, *Dictionary of Mass Communication and Media Research: A Guide for Students, Scholars and Professionals*, (Spokane: Marquette, 2005),143.

16. Patricia Moy, Michael A. Xenos and Verena K. Hess, "Communication and Citizenship: Mapping the Political Effects of Infotainment," *Mass Communication and Society*, 8(2) (2005): 111–131, accessed September 25, 2010, doi: 10.1207/ s15327825mcs0802_3.

17. Matthew Baum, "Soft News and Political Knowledge: Evidence of Absence or Absence of Evidence?" *Political Communication* 20 (2003): 173–190.

18. Postman, *Amusing Ourselves to Death*.

19. See David L. Altheide, "Media Logic and Political Communication," *Political Communication* 21 (2004): 293–296.

20. See Doris A. Graber, "The Infotainment Quotient in Routine Television News," *Discourse and Society* 5 (1994): 483–508.

21. Baym, "Infotainment."

22. Robert W. McChesney and Mike Nichols, *The Death and Life of American Journalism: The Media Revolution That Will Begin the World Again*, (Philadelphia: Nation Books, 2010), 214.

23. Liesbet Van Zoonen, *Entertaining the Citizen: Where Politics and Popular Culture Converge*, (Lanham: Rowman & Littlefield Publishers, 2005), 149.

24. Ibid., 148.

25. Michael Starr, "Jon's Got Game," *New York Post,* September 25, 2008, accessed February 16, 2010, http://www.nypost.com/p/entertainment/tv/item_ARuthNhfE W09txbCOTBNkO;jsessionid=DAC2419E6AF55EAC32A6717A5F8C3954.

26. *Hustler Magazine, Inc. v. Falwell*, 485 U.S. 46 (1988).

27. Robert C. Post, "The Constitutional Concept of Public Discourse: Outrageous Opinion, Democratic Deliberation, and *Hustler Magazine v. Falwell*," *Harvard Law Review* 103, no. 3 (1990): 604.

28. Ibid., 647.

29. John Elster, "Introduction" in *Deliberative Democracy*, (Cambridge: Cambridge University Press, 1998), 1.

10

Media Diversity in the Social Space

Richard Fletcher and Rasmus Kleis Nielsen

Richard Fletcher is a research fellow at the University of Oxford and the lead researcher and co-author of the Digital News Report. *Rasmus Kleis Nielsen is a professor of political communication at the University of Oxford and director of research at the Reuters Institute.*

In this viewpoint, Richard Fletcher and Rasmus Kleis Nielsen examine the algorithmic filtering structures that companies like Facebook, Google, and Twitter employ when distributing content to users. They offer evidence that, contrary to what social media critics argue, the online platform model of news delivery often leads to more diverse media diets. They assert that social media use exposes users to a range of articles from sources with a variety of political perspectives.

D espite widespread fears that social media and other forms of algorithmically-filtered services (like search) lead to filter bubbles, we know surprisingly little about what effect social media have on people's news diets.

Data from the 2017 Reuters Institute *Digital News Report* can help address this. Contrary to conventional wisdom, our analysis shows that social media use is clearly associated with incidental exposure to additional sources of news that people otherwise wouldn't use—and with more politically diverse news diets.

"Using Social Media Appears to Diversify Your News Diet, Not Narrow It," by Richard Fletcher and Rasmus Kleis Nielsen, President and Fellows of Harvard College, June 21, 2017. Published by arrangement with the Nieman Foundation for Journalism.

This matters because distributed discovery—where people find and access news via third parties, like social media, search engines, and increasingly messaging apps—is becoming a more and more important part of how people use media.

The Fear of Filter Bubbles and the End of Incidental Exposure

The role social media plays varies by context and by user. For some highly engaged news lovers, it may be seen as an alternative way of accessing news that allow them to sidestep traditional brands, or as a convenient way of accessing news from multiple sources in one place.

Importantly, however, most people do not consume news online in this way. For them, the Internet—and social media in particular—is just as likely to be a means of passing the time, staying in touch with friends and family, or a source of entertainment.

Some scholars have worried that, in media environments that offer unprecedented choice, people uninterested in news will simply consume something else, with the effect of lowering knowledge, civic engagement, and political participation amongst the population as a whole.

Even for those who are interested enough to pay attention to news on social media, self-selection and ever-more responsive algorithmic selection could combine to trap people inside "filter bubbles," where they only ever see things they like or agree with, from sources they have used in the past. The central fear, as Eli Pariser has put it, is that "news-filtering algorithms narrow what we know."

This, at least, is the theory. These ideas, however, largely fail to take account of the potential for incidental exposure to news on social media: situations where people come across news while using media for other, non-news-related purposes. In the 20th century, incidental exposure was relatively common, as people purchased newspapers to read the non-news content, or left their televisions on between their favorite programs, and in the process, came across news without actively seeking it out. At the beginning of the 21st century, it was hard to see how this could be replicated online, leading people to conclude that incidental exposure would wane. Even as social media reintroduced this potential—by supplementing people's active choices (accessing specific websites) with algorithmic filtering automatically offering up a range of content when people accessed a site or app—the concern was that their underlying logic would have a limiting effect on exposure by giving people more of what they already used and less of other things.

Our evidence, however, suggests that the opposite is happening on social media, at least for now. (The algorithms, of course, continually change.)

Incidental Exposure to News on Social Media

To assess whether distributed discovery leads to filter bubbles or more diverse news diets, we focus on social media, the most important and widely used form of off-site discovery and consumption when it comes to news.

Using data from the 2017 Reuters Institute *Digital News Report,* we divided survey respondents into three non-overlapping groups. One group consists of those who say they intentionally use social media for news. We call them *news users.* Another group are those who do not use social media at all, the *non-users.* Importantly, there is large middle group who *do* use social media, but who in the survey say they *do not* intentionally use it for news. Those we called the *incidentally exposed,* because they might come across news while they use social media for other purposes.[1]

If we compare the number of online news sources used on average in the last week by people within each of these three groups—across the UK, Germany, and the US, three very different media markets—we can see that the incidentally exposed report using more sources of news than people who do not use social media at all. In the US, for example, non-users of social media use on average 1.80 online news sources a week. But this figure rises to 3.29 for those who use social media for purposes other than news, and again to 5.16 for people who intentionally use social media for news. These differences remain statistically significant after controlling for a range of demographic and news attitude variables. (We focus on social media here but have found similar results for other forms of algorithmic filtering like search engines and news aggregators.)

Are Social Media Users Exposed to More of the Same, or to More Diverse Content?

More sources does not necessarily mean *more diverse*. Consuming news from three right-wing sources arguably constitutes a less diverse news diet than from one left-wing and one right-wing source.

But the average number of sources is important to keep in mind. For most ordinary people, incidental exposure to news on social media is associated with a step from using only about one (in the UK and Germany) or two (in the US) online news sources per week to an average of about two (in the UK and Germany) or three (in the US). When dealing with such low numbers, it is likely that *any* increase in the number of sources will necessarily lead to more diverse consumption. Using two right-wing sources is arguably more diverse than using only one.

We can go one step further, however, and measure whether social media users—and especially those incidentally exposed to news while using social media for other purposes—do in fact report using more politically diverse sources of news. We do this by assessing the partisan leanings of different news sources and in turn using this measure to calculate the political diversity of people's news diets.

In each country, we divide news sources into those with a mostly left-leaning audience, and those with a mostly right-leaning audience (with the midpoint the average position on the left-right spectrum amongst the population as a whole).[2] In the US, 43 percent of Huffington Post news users self-identify on the left, compared to just 10 percent on the right, meaning that the news audience for the Huffington Post is to the left of the population as a whole. Conversely, just 9 percent of Fox News online users are left-leaning, and 48 percent are right-leaning. This way, we can use the partisan composition of an outlet's audience as a proxy for its political leaning.

Incidental Exposure Across the Left/Right Divide

With these partisan leanings of individual outlets in mind, we can look at our three groups of social media users (*news users*, those *incidentally exposed* to news on social media, and the *non-users*) and determine the proportion within each group who say they use at least one source from *both* sides of the political spectrum (i.e. from both sides of the "midpoint within country").

Two things are immediately striking. First, the majority in most countries and in most groups do not use sources from across the political spectrum. But also, second, that both social media news users and those incidentally exposed to news on social media not only (a) consume news from more sources but also (b) have a more politically diverse online news diet than those who do not use social media at all. In the US, just 20 percent of those who do not use social media consume news from online brands with left-leaning and right-leaning audiences. Few people, when left to their own devices, opt for a politically diverse news diet. However, the figure rises to 37 percent for those incidentally exposed to news on social media, as they see news links posted by people with different views and different patterns of news consumption. 44 percent of those who use social media for news end up using sources from both the left and the right—more than double the number for non-users. We see the same pattern in both Germany and the UK. Again, these differences remain significant after we control for other factors.

The Future of Distributed Discovery and Filter Bubbles

We have focused here on whether social media use leads to narrow filter bubbles or whether algorithmic filtering in its current forms drives greater diversity through distributed discovery. We have shown that social media use is consistently associated with more, and more diverse, news diets, and that the difference is clear even for the incidentally exposed, those who use social media for other purposes and come across news while doing so. Preliminary analysis of other forms of algorithmic filtering like search engines and news aggregators indicate similar results.

These findings underline that the services offered by powerful platform companies like Facebook and Google, despite what critics fear, may in fact currently contribute to more diverse news diets, rather than narrow filter bubbles. Whether they will still do so after the next algorithm update only they know.

Notes

1. "Non-users" are those that, when surveyed, said that they do not use any of the most popular 15 social networks in each country for any purpose. "News users" are those that said, in follow up questions, that they think of either Facebook, YouTube, or Twitter as a "useful way of getting news" as opposed to "seeing news when using them for other reasons." Everyone else was categorized as the "incidentally exposed," because they use social media, but do not intentionally use it for news

2. All respondents were asked to place themselves on a symmetrical seven-point scale ranging from "very left-wing" to "very right-wing," with the data numerically recoded. All respondents were also asked "which online news brands have you used in the last week" from a list of around the 30 most popular in each country. This data was combined to produce an audience ideology score for each online news brand, with the midpoint determined by the average ideology score of the population as a whole.

11

Media Bias as a Threat to Democratic Governance in the US

Joel S. Hirschhorn

Joel Hirschhorn is a senior official at the Congressional Office of Technology Assessment. He was a professor of political science at the University of Wisconsin–Madison.

Joel Hirschhorn argues that President Trump's antagonism toward the press is simply a byproduct of a thoroughly biased media environment, where much of the criticism leveled at him comes from bad faith and ideologically driven reporting. He argues that the fixation on providing negative coverage of President Trump has prevented coverage of more pressing issues, which in turn has denied viewers and readers access to important information. Hirschhorn claims this has contributed to the "dumbing down" of the news.

Liberals, progressive and Democrats should think critically about the negative impacts of widespread media bias on American democracy. There simply is no doubt that virtually all mainstream media regularly show their strong bias against president Trump and his administration. These media have convinced themselves that they are working to save American democracy from an incompetent, corrupt and dangerous president. And those on the left eat up the negative coverage, which means more money

"Media Bias Just as Threatening as President Trump," by Joel S. Hirschhorn, Counterpunch, August 24, 2017. Reprinted by permission.

for the anti-Trump networks, newspapers and magazines. Never mind that he was elected fairly and legally.

It seems that the leftist media would only be happy if Trump was driven out of office by any means. Such a victory would confirm the undemocratic power of a free press that replaces a military coup with a media one.

Here is my point: More Americans should seriously consider the larger question of whether such a perversion of freedom of the press undermines our democracy. Why? Because instead of fairly presenting genuine news the opinion loaded negative coverage has the goal of bringing down Trump and overturning the election result. The press establishment overwhelmingly filled with liberals and progressives wanted Hillary Clinton and refuse to accept defeat. After all, despite a mighty effort, the media failed to elect Clinton. It continues to seek retribution by bashing Trump and ignoring the many failings of the Clinton campaign.

The press probably feels some responsibility for Trump's success during the primary season. Coverage of Trump's beating up of his Republican opponents was extreme. Now the press is getting even.

To dispel any doubt about the widespread perception of media bias, consider a June 2017 Rasmussen survey of likely American voters. "Fifty percent (50%) think most reporters are biased against the president, up two points from January. Just four percent (4%) think most reporters are biased in Trump's favor. Given the president's testy relationship with the media, however, it's not surprising that 76% of Republicans and 51% of voters not affiliated with either major political party believe most reporters are biased against the president, a view shared by only 24% of Democrats." Perhaps the most important finding is that "Nearly 90% of voters who Strongly Approve of the job the president is doing think most reporters are biased against Trump and rate media coverage of him as poor."

These results support the view that all the negative coverage may strengthen the Trump base, which largely have stopped reading and listening to what they think is fake news. News based on reporting of facts has been replaced by opinion and a near total emphasis on what Trump says rather than on what he and his administration have done. In other words, rhetoric preempts accomplishments, and those positive accomplishments from a conservative perspective are also viewed negatively by the leftist press. Information about governance is purposely kept out of the media limelight to allow Trump rhetoric to get endless vicious criticism.

Often, such surveys are dismissed. So consider the 2017 study prepared by the Shorenstein Center on Media, Politics, and Public Policy at Harvard. It revealed what reasonable people would consider a disturbing level of media bias against president Trump. Here are the fractions of negative news coverage towards Trump: CNN and NBC, 93%; CBS, 91%; *New York Times*, 87%; *Washington Post*, 83%. FOX had the most equal coverage, with 52% negative.

Those who like the biased anti-Trump media coverage should reflect on how all that coverage robs them of getting solid information on myriad local, state and world events. In other words, the biased media dominance inevitably leads to a dumbing down of the public about what is really happening that merits news coverage as well as details about what is happening in the sphere of public policy. Journalism itself has been degraded to such a degree that for much of the population no one believes anything coming from the opinion-loaded media. Apologists for the left and right unload opinions rather than enlightening information and analysis. Rational people do not trust the press.

The core issue is whether the press is giving itself too much credit for presenting the truth. In fact, what is happening is the presentation of opinion not objective facts that reveal the truth. Truth requires objectivity and a concerted emphasis on undisputed facts. Instead, opinion, even in so-called news stories, is routinely presented.

Biased media hiding behind freedom of the press should disgust all Americans. We all are being robbed of huge amounts of news and information. Amazingly, for example, network CBS news used its whole hour broadcast to presenting anti-Trump laced coverage of the recent Charlottsville event. That is virtually a nightly occurrence at CNN where only anti-Trump diatribes are presented in multiple shows. The front pages of the main newspapers are the same. Real news from all over the country and the world is not given to the public the way it used to be.

The credibility of the media has taken a lethal blow. What they deem good for their business now will ultimately backfire as Americans for years to come seek and find alternative news sources or eliminate news from their lives. A truly informed public is needed for a quality democracy, and we are losing that.

Yes, a free press is vital for democracy. But a deeply biased press is not.

As to these crazy times, Ruben Navarrette Jr. summed them eloquently: "President Trump and the media deserve each other. Both are driven by ego and take criticism personally. Both will twist the facts to defend themselves and push their agenda. … Americans are fed precooked narratives by the Fourth Estate. We're told what's important and what isn't, what to focus on and what to ignore, and—above all—what to think. …I sure miss journalism." So many of us do.

12

When Politicians and Candidates Antagonize the News Media

David Greenberg

David Greenberg is a professor of journalism and media studies at Rutgers University. He is the author of Nixon's Shadow, *which discusses how Nixon's presidency transformed how we think of the presidency, as well as the biography* Calvin Coolidge.

In this excerpted viewpoint, David Greenberg examines the cynical strategy behind President Trump's persistent hostility toward reporters and the news media in general. He suggests that the current atmosphere may be a symptom, rather than part of the cause, of the news media's diminishing authority in American culture. Adversarial reporting has caused the public to lose faith in the news media, and stabs at President Trump come across as petty rather than informative.

D onald Trump's attacks on the news media since taking office have been so persistent, so over-the-top, so deranged—in a word, so Trumpian—that it's not surprising to see a backlash. Journalists are denouncing Trump for his continuous stream of vitriol toward them. Newspapers and magazines are enjoying spikes in subscriptions and support. Around 200 activists even congregated in Times Square one Sunday in February to show solidarity with the press corps against Trump's onslaught.

"There's a Logic to Trump's War on the Media," by David Greenberg, the American Prospect, April 28, 2017. Reprinted by permission.

The press's job of keeping the public well informed about national and international affairs is no doubt harder than ever today. Trump's eagerness to attack the media relentlessly and without restraint has made it harder still. But the ultimate reason that a demagogue like Trump mounts such crude, broad-brush attacks is that the institutional power of the press has diminished, and Trump descries political advantage in putting more pressure on them.

In 2017, the news media command considerably less authority than they once did to set the news agenda, arbitrate disputes over public issues, or even establish a common standard of what we ought to be discussing. Seeing that weakness, Trump appears to believe that he doesn't need the mainstream media the way his predecessors did—and that when it comes to raw, open warfare with the journalists who cover him, he has nothing to lose. Whether he is right or wrong will depend on the performance of the press in the next four years.

The Nixon Precedent

When we hear the young Trump administration described as "unprecedented" in its treatment of the media, we often forget that all presidents spar with the press, often viciously. Almost every administration in modern times—since the rise of an influential press corps in the early 20th century—has at some point been labeled the "worst ever" in its treatment of the fourth estate, only to have such florid overstatements debunked in the light of history.

But if there is one close parallel with Trump in recent presidential history, it is with Richard Nixon, generally considered the president most unfriendly to the news media until now. Like Trump, Nixon hated the press for two very different reasons, one political, the other personal.

The political argument, stoked by aides like Pat Buchanan and Roger Ailes who preached a cultural populism, was that America's elite newsrooms and television networks were riddled with liberals who promote an ideological agenda or at least let their opinions color their reporting. A familiar right-wing talking point today, this claim was relatively novel in the 1960s. But it gained traction during that tumultuous decade thanks to coverage of events ranging from the civil rights protests to the riots at the 1968 Democratic convention. Nixon embraced this view from the start of his presidency. In 1969, his vice president, Spiro Agnew, entered the history books with a pair of speeches assailing the bias of the leading news organizations. Over the years, the "liberal media" claim did yeoman's work for the rising conservative movement. It mobilized an angry base of scapegoat-hungry voters and simultaneously helped to discredit any news or commentary critical of the conservative movement's leaders or ideas.

If ideology fed Nixon's attack on the press as biased, it was personal animus that gave the attack its nasty bite. A self-described "paranoiac," with deep resentments that spawned an extravagant sense of entitlement, Nixon saw enemies everywhere. At least since his 1952 slush-fund scandal, when he almost had to step down as Dwight Eisenhower's vice presidential running mate, he had been convinced that the press corps had it in for him. Aides commented that he couldn't distinguish legitimate criticisms or even routine questioning from personal animus.

The result was a self-fulfilling prophecy: Regarding journalists as the enemy, President Nixon punished or lashed out at them in myriad ways. But the more he did so, the more aggressively they went after him, thus validating his suspicions. Watergate in particular confirmed many reporters' resolve to practice what came to be called "adversarial journalism." Sometimes this adversarial posture was channeled into hard-hitting, critical reportage. During the ensuing decades, however, it increasingly appeared as gratuitous scandal-mongering, snide and captious television punditry, or overblown feeding frenzies over small-bore pseudo-scandals. The result was to damage the press corps' standing with not only conservatives but voters of all stripes.

Trump Versus Nixon

With Trump's election we have another president who regards the media as both politically and personally hostile. Like Nixon, Trump harbors an irrepressible sense of victimization, an ego insecurity that's momentarily salved by eruptions of rage at those—especially in the media—who cross him, question him, or draw attention to his failings. Like Nixon, Trump's insecurity leads him to monitor the news obsessively, creating endless occasions for explosions of anger.

But Nixon's and Trump's personalities aren't identical. Nixon cultivated the illusion that he was a straight arrow, a schoolboy, a square. Sometimes the mask slipped—such as at his famous "last press conference" in 1962, when, possibly inebriated, he excoriated reporters for giving him "the shaft" during his just-concluded failed bid for governor of California. Outbursts like these, though not uncommon, were nonetheless jarring, because the private Nixon suddenly on view was at odds with the statesmanlike persona he normally labored to project.

When it came to retaliating against the press, Nixon was if anything worse than Trump (at least so far). Not only did he mete out petty punishments, like preventing a journalist who was investigating his finances from going on his historic trip to China, but he abused his power in unconstitutional ways. Nixon had the FBI investigate enemies and the IRS audit them; he tried to deny broadcast licenses to the Washington Post Company as political payback; he put reporters under surveillance.

Notably, though, these measures were mostly concealed. In public, Nixon strove, though not always successfully, to adhere to the norms of civil discourse. Asked about growing sentiment for impeachment at a news conference as the Watergate scandal spiraled out of control, he delivered a barbed joke: "Well, I am glad we don't take the vote of this room." Later, when asked if he had been lambasting the TV networks out of anger, he replied, "Don't get the impression that you arouse my anger. … You see, one can only be angry with those he respects." Though his bitterness was palpable, Nixon remained the collegiate debater, trying to score rhetorical points.

Trump doesn't seem to care about seeming respectable. He revels in his bad-boy persona. Whereas Nixon's private White House tapes shocked Americans by revealing a petty, vulgar vindictiveness at variance with his public mien, Trump's "Access Hollywood" tape, in which he bragged about grabbing women's genitals, didn't seem to shame him or deter his voters, who were already familiar with his lecherous, alpha-male posturings. For all the attention it garnered, the tape didn't reveal a Trump fundamentally different from the one we already knew.

When it comes to the press, therefore, Trump has made no bones about waging war. His attacks aren't necessarily more dangerous than Nixon's, but they are more personal, crude, impulsive, and indiscriminate. In public, Trump has outstripped his predecessor in calling journalists names and questioning their honesty. When CNN reported on, and Buzzfeed then published, a dossier of opposition research compiled against Trump, he called Buzzfeed "a failing pile of garbage" at a news conference— pausing as if to search for a better epithet but grabbing the one closest to his lips, no matter how juvenile. Blurring the distinction between CNN's reported and carefully worded story and Buzzfeed's indiscriminate information dump, Trump then called CNN's report "fake news"—a term that has become his administration's favorite phrase to try to discredit any news, accurate or not, that it doesn't like. When the network's Jim Acosta tried to respond, Trump shut him down, saying, "I am not going to give you a question. You are fake news." These salvos exhibit neither Nixon's desire to remain decorous nor his instinct to win the argument. They're pure invective and insult—the unadulterated expression of anger and enmity and Trump's own need simply to insist that he's right.

[…]

Weakened Warriors

But the key factor that has enabled Trump to adopt his gonzo style is the loss of power by the fourth estate. Since Nixon's day, the cultural authority of the mainstream news media has plummeted. It's now simply much harder for journalists to gain a hearing with the broad slice of the public that used to trust what they reported. As a result, their efforts to correct Trump's misinformation, highlight problems in his presidency, or even report on corruption, scandal, and dysfunction have to swim against the tide if they are to reach the huge swaths of the electorate who trust Trump more than they trust the press.

Several long-term developments have weakened the press institutionally. The prevalence of adversarial reporting (especially in the form of crude gotcha journalism as opposed to substantive investigation) diminished reporters in the public eye. To many citizens, regardless of ideology, the typical Washington journalist now seemed preening, self-important, and unremittingly negative. The explosion of armchair television punditry, at the expense of reporting, had a similar effect.

Another blow came with proliferation first of cable TV news and then of internet blogs and start-up webzines. The multitude of outlets scattered the news-consuming public's attentions, further chipping away at the authority once commanded by news-gathering reporters at blue-chip newspapers and sober-minded television anchors at the big networks. The cable channels and new websites could also filch the heart of a story from the top-tier news outlets and serve it up to younger or more casual readers in a snarky package, blurring the line between reportage and parasitical commentary. Twitter has exacerbated the tendency to parasitism, allowing commentators of varying degrees of knowledge and talent to opine about news gathered by others; it has also increased the emphasis on snark, as purportedly neutral Washington reporters—men and women who are expected to banish any hint of editorializing from their news stories—dispense with professionalism to spin out sassy, hostile, nit-picking, pompous, and ill-informed opinions, whether about Trump or anything else that pops up on their phones.

And then there was the 40-year right-wing drumbeat about the mainstream media's purported liberal bias, which convinced many conservatives not to trust sources like the *New York Times* or the network news shows—outlets that, not long ago, were widely recognized as neutral and nonpartisan bearers of information. In the 1990s came the rise in quick succession of talk radio, Fox News, and countless right-wing internet sites. These outlets amounted to a full menu of alternative news sources providing conservatives with counter-arguments and ripostes to any judgments proffered in the mainstream media, which, increasingly, they felt license to ignore.

During George W. Bush's presidency, this undertaking expanded to construct a kind of alternate reality for the right. Under Bush, the conservative movement consummated a decades-long degradation of experts—in economics, science, law, intelligence, and other fields—on whom journalists had long depended to help readers make reliable sense of the world. Experts who doubted the administration's claims, whether about Iraq's nuclear weapons program, global warming, or Bush's own economic policies, were themselves dismissed as partisans who cloaked their political conclusions in the trappings of disinterested expertise. Observers wryly labeled Bush's presidency "postmodern," in which no fixed truth existed and all arguments were reduced to their political utility.

Already, early in the new century, some were speaking of a "post-truth" society. Others used pretentious coinages like "epistemic closure" to explain the imperviousness of tightly knit ideological communities—now often forged online—to countervailing evidence. But in the following decade, things got worse still. Not just in the usual shadowy corners of society but increasingly out in the open, outré conspiracy theories now flourished—the most infamous of them being the slander that Barack Obama wasn't born in the United States. As the conservative but anti-Trump radio host Charlie Sykes wrote, "The echo chamber had morphed into a full-blown alternate reality silo of conspiracy theories, fake news and propaganda." Where Cold War delusions, like the supposed communist plot to fluoridate our water, could be sidelined by media gatekeepers, now worldwide interconnectedness allows nonsense to spread far and wide. Pseudo-scandals like Benghazi gripped not just the usual smattering of crackpots who had spun scenarios about the Kennedy assassination or Roswell but also ranking members of Congress, influential voices in the right-wing mediasphere, and individuals on Twitter who managed to build up large and loyal followings—including, of course, Donald Trump.

The Road Back

Reporters now face the challenge of regaining the trust of citizens on the left as well as the right. These disaffected Americans no longer seem hungry for the old meal of straight-up reported news with a twist of analysis and a side of opinion. They prefer other fare: the ideological reinforcements of the cable news ranters; the self-congratulatory humor and sputtering indignation of the comedy anchors; the alternate universes of the social media conspiracists; or simply the generalized noise of the internet. Instead of rebuilding their credibility, some journalists seem to be chasing these audiences by emulating sites like *BuzzFeed* and the *Huffington Post* instead of the *Times* and the *Post*. The *Times* seems poised to make the potentially fatal mistake of cutting back on editing. The snark-filled tweets of reporters—who act as if they're joking in the breakroom rather than speaking for the papers of record—further chip away at their authority. Still other ostensibly fair-minded reporters, lured by the cameras, slip out of the temperate personas they don for PBS or Charlie Rose and take potshots at the president on MSNBC. This approach will never win back the readers who are seeking uncolored, trustworthy information. Confronted with the cacophony of fury and complaint that floods the airwaves and fills the screens, Trump and his supporters can write it off as "so much anger and hatred."

Understandably, journalists who feel targeted by Trump want to fight back. But their counterpunching won't be effective if it's perceived as either self-aggrandizing or partisan. For more than a century, American journalism has thrived by placing reporting over ideology. The most persuasive rebuttal to the right wing's "liberal media" claim has always been the simple fact of the press's overriding professionalism. In the world of the mainstream media, where journalists aspire to be objective and nonpartisan, all the professional rewards and incentives—prizes, prestige, advertising dollars, personal satisfactions—accrue not to those who spout off in news columns or land a punch against a political target, but to those who dig up big news, uncover secrets, and score scoops. Not every individual journalist has necessarily articulated this understanding of what keeps them on the straight and narrow, but most follow it nonetheless. Lately, however, it seems that fewer reporters appreciate the value of upholding traditional journalistic norms and are in danger of sacrificing long-held principles for the short-term satisfaction of getting in a jab at Trump.

There are ways to fight back that can enhance the press's standing rather than lowering it. Instead of hollering about being called an "enemy of the people," a reporter can explain to readers the distinctive and fraught history of that phrase, as Andrew Higgins of the *New York Times* did. Instead of crying "liar" when Trump falsely claims that three million people voted illegally, a newspaper can track down the source of that fictitious statistic, as the *Guardian* did back in December, and explain how it reached the president-elect's ears.

Even more important, reporters have dug deep into the burgeoning Russia scandal, the backgrounds of Trump's cabinet nominees, the disarray behind his misguided immigration ban, and other big developments of the administration's early days. Context and clarifying information, not outrage, is what journalists can produce to keep the public informed and restore their position as sources of reliable news.

Twelve days into the Trump presidency, Reuters editor-in-chief Steve Adler issued a memo to his staff noting the "challenging" environment for journalists, in which the president had already called them "among the most dishonest human beings on earth" and his chief strategist, Steve Bannon, called the media "the opposition party." But instead of boycotting administration briefings or trying to rally support for the press, he said, Reuters would redouble its commitment "to reporting fairly and honestly, by doggedly gathering hard-to-get information—and by remaining impartial."

The big unanswered question, though, is whether reporting out the facts and bringing to light new information will in the current media environment sway any of those who've given up on the mainstream media. Some may be hunkered in right-wing mediaspheres, where suspicions or the leading media institutions, bolstered daily by Trump's cries of fake news, prove an insurmountable barrier to changing minds. Others are scattered in their attentions, unwilling or unable to devote the time to sorting claims from counterclaims.

History again provides perspective, and maybe hope. In previous times, similar problems existed, if not to the same degree. During Watergate, the White House and other skeptical voices initially dismissed the scandal as what Donald Trump would call fake news. But in time, the reporting of a small few penetrated the right-wing bubbles. "At the beginning, all of us assumed Watergate was ... what Ron Ziegler told us it was," wrote William F. Buckley: "nothing more than a third-rate burglary." But in time, the scales fell from Buckley's eyes, and he came to think that those who stood by Nixon did so "because the alternative is to wake up in the morning and find that they are in agreement with a particular conclusion reached by the *New York Times*." Even many of them changed their minds by the end.

In the coming four years, reporting will count for more than ever. Whether Donald Trump turns out to be an overgrown child or a fearsome menace, a proto-fascist or a paper tiger, it seems clear already that a lot of journalists are determined—not in the spitball wars of Twitter or the food-fights of the cable news shows, but in the great gray columns of newsprint that are necessary to set forth a story in full—to put up a fight.

Organizations to Contact

The editors have compiled the following list of organizations concerned with the issues debated in this book. The descriptions are derived from materials provided by the organizations. All have publications or information available for interested readers. The list was compiled on the date of publication of the present volume; the information provided here may change. Be aware that many organizations take several weeks or longer to respond to inquiries, so allow as much time as possible.

American Press Institute
4401 N. Fairfax Drive, Suite 300
Arlington, VA 22203
(571) 366-1200
email: hello@pressinstitute.org
website: www.americanpressinstitute.org

The American Press Institute advances an innovative and sustainable news industry by helping publishers understand and engage with audiences, grow revenue, improve public-service journalism, and succeed at organizational change.

Digital Media Association (DiMA)
1050 17th Street NW, Suite 520
Washington, DC 20036
(202) 639-9509
website: www.digmedia.org

DiMA is the ambassador for the digital media industry: webcasters, online media, digital services, and technology innovators. DiMA is the leading advocate for a stable legal environment in which it is possible to build ideas into industries, and inventions into profits.

FactCheck.org

202 S. 36th Street
Philadelphia, PA 19104-3806
(215) 898-9400
email: editor@factcheck.org
website: www.factcheck.org

FactCheck.org is a project of the Annenberg Public Policy Center of the University of Pennsylvania. It is a nonpartisan, nonprofit "consumer advocate" for voters that aims to reduce the level of deception and confusion in US politics. It monitors the factual accuracy of what is said by major US political players in the form of TV ads, debates, speeches, interviews, and news releases.

Fairness and Accuracy in Reporting (FAIR)

124 W. 30th Street, Suite 201
New York, NY 10001
(212) 633-6700
email: fair@fair.org
website: www.fair.org

FAIR, the national media watch group, has been offering well-documented criticism of media bias and censorship since 1986.

Freedom of the Press Foundation

601 Van Ness Avenue, Suite E731
San Francisco, CA 94102
website: www.freedom.press

The Freedom of the Press Foundation is a nonprofit organization dedicated to helping support and defend public-interest journalism focused on exposing mismanagement, corruption, and law-breaking in government. It works to preserve and strengthen the rights guaranteed to the press under the First Amendment through crowdfunding, digital security, and internet advocacy.

News Media Alliance

4401 N. Fairfax Drive, Suite 300
Arlington, VA 22203
(571) 366-1000
email: info@newsmediaalliance.org
website: www.newsmediaalliance.org

The News Media Alliance is a nonprofit organization headquartered in Washington, DC. The organization was founded in 1992 through a merger of seven associations serving the newspaper industry and was originally known as the Newspaper Association of America (NAA).

Pew Research Center – Journalism and Media Center

1615 L Street NW, Suite 800
Washington, DC 20036
(202) 419-4300
website: www.journalism.org

The Pew Research Center is a distinguished polling and research organization that focuses on politics, media, and social scientific issues.

PolitiFact

1100 Connecticut Avenue NW, Suite 440
Washington, DC 20036
(202) 463-0571
http://www.politifact.com

PolitiFact is a fact-checking website that rates the accuracy of claims by elected officials and others who speak up in American politics.

Reuters Institute for the Study of Journalism
University of Oxford
13 Norham Gardens
Oxford OX2 6PS
United Kingdom
email: reuters.institute@politics.ox.ac.uk
website: https://reutersinstitute.politics.ox.ac.uk

The Reuters Institute for the Study of Journalism is a globally focused research center at the University of Oxford, working to track the world's media and its trends, developments, and forecasts.

Society of Professional Journalists (SPJ)
Eugene S. Pulliam National Journalism Center
3909 N. Meridian Street, Suite 200
Indianapolis, IN 46208
(317) 927-8000
email: info@spj.org
website: www.spj.org

The Society of Professional Journalists is dedicated to the perpetuation of a free press as the cornerstone of the United States and the liberty of its citizens.

Bibliography

Books

Eric Alterman, *What Liberal Media? The Truth About Bias and the News.* Cambridge, MA: Basic Books, 2003.

Larry Atkins, *Skewed: A Critical Thinker's Guide to Media Bias.* New York, NY: Prometheus Books, 2016.

Sharyl Attkisson, *The Smear: How Shady Political Operatives and Fake News Control What You See, What You Think, and How You Vote.* New York, NY: HarperCollins Publishers, 2017.

Bruce Bartlett, *The Truth: A Citizen's Guide to Separating Facts from Lies and Stopping Fake News in Its Tracks.* New York, NY: Ten Speed Press, 2017.

Matt Carlson, *Journalistic Authority: Legitimating News in the Digital Era.* New York, NY: Columbia University Press, 2017.

Timothy E. Cook, *Governing with the News: The News Media as a Political Institution.* Chicago, IL: University of Chicago Press, 2005.

Bernard Goldberg, *Bias: A CBS Insider Exposes How the Media Distort the News.* Washington, DC: Regnery Publishing, Inc., 2002.

Jim A. Kuypers, *Partisan Journalism: A History of Media Bias in the United States.* Lanham, MD: Rowman & Littlefield Publishing Group, 2014.

Matthew Levendusky, *How Partisan Media Polarize America.* Chicago, IL: University of Chicago Press. 2013

Daniel J. Levitin, *Weaponized Lies: How to Think Critically in the Post-Truth Era.* New York, NY: Dutton, 2016.

Thomas M. Nichols, *The Death of Expertise: The Campaign Against Established Knowledge and Why It Matters.* New York, NY: Oxford University Press, 2017.

Neil Postman, *Amusing Ourselves to Death: Public Discourse in the Age of Show Business.* New York, NY: Penguin Books, 1985.

Bob Schieffer and H. Andrew Schwartz, *Overload: Finding the Truth in Today's Deluge of News.* Lanham, MD: Rowman & Littlefield Publishing Group, 2017.

Adam J. Schiffer. *Evaluating Media Bias.* Lanham, MD: Rowman & Littlefield Publishing Group, 2018.

Bruce J. Schulman and Julian E. Zelizer, eds., *Media Nation: The Political History of News in Modern America.* Philadelphia, PA: University of Pennsylvania Press, 2017.

Gabriel Sherman, *The Loudest Voice in the Room: How the Brilliant, Bombastic Roger Ailes Built FOX News—and Divided a Country.* New York, NY: Random House, 2014.

Periodicals and Internet Sources

Matthew A. Baum and Tim Groeling, "New Media and the Polarization of American Political Discourse," *Political Communication*, 2008. https://sites.hks.harvard.edu/fs/mbaum/documents/BaumGroeling_NewMedia.pdf.

Timothy P. Carney, "Liberal News Media Bias Has a Serious Effect, *New York Times*, December 21, 2015. https://www.nytimes.com/roomfordebate/2015/11/11/why-has-trust-in-the-news-media-declined/liberal-news-media-bias-has-a-serious-effect.

Sarah Childress, "Study: Election Coverage Skewed by 'Journalistic Bias,'" *PBS Frontline*, July 12, 2016. https://www.pbs.org/wgbh/frontline/article/study-election-coverage-skewed-by-journalistic-bias.

Robert M. Entman, "Media Framing Biases and Political Power: Explaining Slant in News Coverage of 2008 Campaign," Sage Journals, August 17, 2010. http://journals.sagepub .com/doi/abs/10.1177/1464884910367587.

David Folkenflik, "The Birth of FOX News," *Salon*, October 19, 2013. https://www.salon.com/2013/10/19/the_birth_of_ fox_news.

Ted Genoways, "The Problem of Coastal Media Bias in Covering Middle America," *New Republic*, December 8, 2017. https://newrepublic.com/article/146176/problem -coastal-media-bias-covering-middle-america.

Marc Gunther, "The Transformation of Network News: How Profitability Has Moved Networks Out of Hard News," Nieman Reports, June 15, 1999. http://niemanreports.org /articles/the-transformation-of-network-news.

Glenn Halbrooks, "How TV News Has Evolved in the Past 50 Years," *Balance*, June 26, 2017. https://www.thebalance.com /a-look-at-tv-news-history-over-the-past-50-years-2315217.

Amanda Hess, "How to Escape Your Political Bubble for a Clearer View," *New York Times*, March 3, 2017. https://www .nytimes.com/2017/03/03/arts/the-battle-over-your -political-bubble.html.

Ezra Klein, "Something Is Breaking American Politics, But It's Not Social Media," Vox, April 12, 2017. https://www.vox .com/policy-and-politics/2017/4/12/15259438/social -media-political-polarization.

Matthew Levendusky, "Partisan Media and Polarization: Challenges for Future Work," *Oxford Research Encyclopedia of Politics*, January 2017. https://web.sas.upenn.edu/mleven /files/2016/10/ORE_Partisan_Media_Chapter-1ue372j.pdf.

Amy Mitchell, Jeffrey Gottfried, Jocelyn Kiley, and Katerina Eva Matsa, "Political Polarization & Media Habits," Pew Research Center, October 21, 2014. http://www.journalism .org/2014/10/21/political-polarization-media-habits.

Brendan Nyhan, "Relatively Few Americans Live in Partisan Media Bubble, But They're Influential," *New York Times*, September 7, 2016. https://www.nytimes.com/2016/09/08 /upshot/relatively-few-people-are-partisan-news -consumers-but-theyre-influential.html?_r=0.

Will Oremus, "The Filter Bubble Revisited," Slate, April 5, 2017. http://www.slate.com/articles/technology /technology/2017/04/filter_bubbles_revisited_the_internet_ may_not_be_driving_political_polarization.html.

Jack Shafer and Tucker Doherty, "The Media Bubble Is Worse Than You Think," *Politico Magazine*, May/June 2017. https:// www.politico.com/magazine/story/2017/04/25/media -bubble-real-journalism-jobs-east-coast-215048.

Art Swift, "Six in 10 in U.S. See Partisan Bias in News Media," Gallup News, April 5, 2017. http://news.gallup.com /poll/207794/six-partisan-bias-news-media.aspx.

Index

E

Elements of Journalism, The, 19, 24
Elster, John, 88

F

Facebook, 9, 65, 94, 99
Fairchild Publications, 30
Fearon, James, 89
Fili-Krushel, Pat, 78
filter bubbles, 94, 95–96, 99
Fleischmann, Raoul, 29
Fletcher, Richard, 94–99
Fox News, 8, 30, 42, 98, 110
FreedomWorks, 41
Friedman, Paul, 78

G

Gannett, 30
General Electric, 26, 32, 33, 73
Gingrich, Newt, 43
Goldwater, Barry, 48
Google, 28, 62, 94, 99
Greenberg, David, 104–113
Grunwald, Henry, 26
Gunther, Marc, 72–82

H

Hannity, Sean, 41, 48
Heritage Action, 41
Hewitt, Don, 74–75, 80
Heyward, Andrew, 75, 76–77
Hirschhorn, Joel S., 100–103
Huckabee, Mike, 41, 47

I

Ingraham, Laura, 41, 45, 48
It's Even Worse Than It Looks, 43

J

Jennings, Peter, 80, 81
Jindal, Bobby, 41
Johnson, James, 89
Jones, Jeffrey, 52, 53, 54
journalism
    and comedy, 50–58
    ethical issues in, 7, 19–24

K

Kabaservice, Geoffrey, 42
Kalb, Marvin, 73
Karmazin, Mel, 73
Katz, Elihu, 56
Kennedy, Dan, 83–86
Kille, Leighton Walter, 19–24
Klein, Ezra, 9
Knight-Ridder, 30
Koppel, Ted, 57, 79, 80, 81

L

Larris, Rachel Joy, 50–58
Larry King Live, 74
Levin, Gerald, 27
Levin, Mark, 41
Lewis, Peter H., 83
Limbaugh, Rush, 41, 42
Lott, Trent, 45
Luce, Henry, 28